P9-DED-491

The Unsung Season

BOOKS BY SYDNEY EDDISON

A PATCHWORK GARDEN
Unexpected Pleasures from a Country Garden

A PASSION FOR DAYLILIES
The Flowers and the People

THE UNSUNG SEASON
Gardens and Gardeners in Winter

The Unsung Season

GARDENS AND GARDENERS IN WINTER

Sydney Eddison

Photographs by Karen Bussolini

HOUGHTON MIFFLIN COMPANY   *Boston • New York*   1995

Copyright © 1995 by Sydney Eddison
Photographs copyright © 1995 by Karen Bussolini
All rights reserved

For information about permission to reproduce selections from
this book, write to Permissions, Houghton Mifflin Company,
215 Park Avenue South, New York, New York 10003.

For information about this and other Houghton Mifflin trade
and reference books and multimedia products, visit The Bookstore
at Houghton Mifflin on the World Wide Web
at http://www.hmco.com/trade/.

Library of Congress Cataloging-in-Publication Data

Eddison, Sydney, date.
    The unsung season : gardens and gardeners in winter / Sydney
Eddison; photographs by Karen Bussolini.
        p.   cm.
    Includes bibliographical references (p.   ) and index.
    ISBN 0-395-71551-2 (alk. paper)
    1. Winter gardening. I. Title.
SB439.5.E33   1995
635.9 — dc20   95-4921 CIP

Printed in the United States of America

Book design by Robert Overholtzer

QUM 10 9 8 7 6 5 4 3 2 1

For my unsung partner and husband, Martin

— S.E.

For John and Jackson

— K.B.

Acknowledgments

We are deeply indebted to the subjects of this book. We would like to thank them for sharing their stories, their enthusiasm, and their expertise. Besides giving of themselves and their time, they often fed and sometimes housed us. Again and again they proved that what you hear about the generosity of gardeners is absolutely true. Our heartfelt thanks to one and all. Karen would especially like to thank Ned and Betsy Williams, Gary and Sarah Milek, Joanna Reed, Ann Sims, and Ellie Casey for providing comfort, sustenance, and friendship.

We would also like to thank Gregory Piotrowski of the New York Botanical Garden for checking botanical nomenclature and Martha McKeon for helping with the appendix. In addition, Trudy Bancroft, Mary Ann McGourty, and Marnie Flook provided invaluable tips, information, and inspiration.

We are grateful to our editor, Frances Tenenbaum, for the opportunity to do the book and to our agents, Helen Pratt and Caroline Press, who facilitated our work and took a lively interest in the project.

Last but far from least, there are those who watch and wait: Karen's husband, John Scofield, and son, Jackson, who kept the home fires burning and the laundry done while she traveled the northern latitudes, and my own ever-patient spouse.

Contents

Introduction

In 1992, Karen Bussolini began a photographic record of my Connecticut garden through the seasons. The garden is a presence for twelve months of the year and in full view of the most lived-in rooms in our house. In pastel spring or the heavy green of summer, surrounded by blazing fall colors or revealed in the stark simplicity of winter, it is part of the landscape. For this reason and because my husband and I live here year-round, I wanted a year-round garden. A lot of trial and error has gone into this effort over the past thirty-odd years, but now there is something to look at in every season. It was this aspect of the garden that attracted Karen and her camera.

Garden pleasures don't stop when the leaves fall. Some of the most beautiful and startling effects result from this annual phenomenon. I particularly welcome the spacious sky. Surrounded as we are by woodland, the summer sky shrinks to an island of blue in a sea of green foliage. At dusk, an invisible sun slides behind the screen of overlapping leaves. But in the winter we have topaz sunsets visible through an intricate network of bare branches, and we can see the shape and contours of the countryside.

Below us to the east, the land falls away to the frozen desert of Lake Lillinonah, silent at last after a summer of speedboats and water skiers. To the north and west, the terrain rises steadily. Stripped of its leafy understory, the woodland separates into individual trees with straight black trunks. Maples, oaks, and tulip trees — rank upon rank of them — mount the ridge, part of New England's rocky spine.

Twenty miles farther north along the same ridge, Karen, her husband, John Scofield, and their young son watch the sun go down across Hatch Pond. It sinks into a long, low wave of wooded hills — green in the summer, blue in the winter. At their backs, a skyscraper of exposed rock soars upward for fifty feet or more. Their developing garden lies athwart the steep slope below the cliff. The site is daunting, but the views are magnificent. John has hacked alcoves out of the hillside and built log benches to take advantage of the panorama below. The family has ambitious plans for a system of paths to traverse the almost vertical slope; sure-footed deer have already established the best routes.

As Karen took photos in our garden, we discovered many bonds. Although I have a twenty-year head start, we have similar memories of growing up in the country, roaming the woods, and loving wildflowers. Nutmeggers born and bred, we have continued to live and garden in rural Connecticut for most of our lives. Even our gardens share common ground, physically linked as they are by the same ancient mountain chain.

Gardens brought us together, and as the photographic record unfolded and the months passed, we began to think about doing a book. At first we toyed with the notion of a four-season chronicle of my garden, but we abandoned the project as too limited in scope. However, the seasonal theme haunted us both. Then Karen hit on it: "Why not winter gardens?" And, as an afterthought, "Gardens and gardeners in winter." I was instantly riveted. The idea was as fresh and invigorating as the season. Gardens and gardeners leapt to mind.

I thought of Jack and June Dunbar's New York City garden. Divided by modular decking into beds and borders, it is richly planted with hollies, camellias, and rhododendrons. The focal point is a fastigiate weeping beech. As marvelous in twig as in leaf, it was delivered by truck on the street side of their brownstone and had to be brought into the garden through a neighbor's bedroom. Jack, an interior designer and painter, was clear in his mind about wanting this tree especially for its winter aspect. Upright forms draw the attention skyward, but he wanted his eye to rove up and down the long, graceful lines of the dependant branches.

On the opposite side of Central Park from the Dunbars' garden is the much admired Conservatory Garden, restored by Lynden B. Miller. As a designer of public gardens, Lynden has managed to make large, unremarkable spaces seem charming and personal. Her northwestern Connecticut garden was the laboratory in which she developed and refined her approach to garden-making. Here, as in her public work, she combines romantic abundance with crisp discipline.

Winter reveals both aspects of Lynden's signature style in the design of her garden. Imagine a perfectly groomed semicircular hedge of black-green yew and, against it, beds well furnished with red-twig dogwoods and sheaves of parchment-colored ornamental grass; dwarf blue spruces and globes of twiggy barberry, clipped so their shapes contrast with the horizontals of hedge, fence, and distant hills. Dust it all with snow, and you have a stunning sight.

The more I thought about gardens and gardeners in winter, the more the topic intrigued me. Gardeners seemed to tumble over one another, demanding inclusion — gifted plantsmen and plantswomen who make the cold months come alive with vegetative beauty. Polly Hill's seed-grown arboretum on Martha's Vineyard, Massachusetts, boasts an extraordinary conifer collection, including handsome Japanese umbrella pine, which has whorls of flat dark-green needles, just made to catch pompoms of snow. In addition there are berried shrubs, deciduous trees with patterned bark, and a ravishing arbor of European hornbeam (*Carpinus betulus*). In winter, the intricate vaulting of the bare, interlacing branches forms an airy tunnel.

For years, gardening friends and acquaintances had been telling me about Joanna Reed. This remarkable woman singlehandedly tends a huge and fascinating garden in Malvern, Pennsylvania. For fifty years she has been enjoying the "constant surprises and discoveries" that the winter garden affords. To add color and form and to bring birds to the garden, she deliberately leaves standing the dried flower heads and seedpods of certain perennials.

"The showiest," she says, "is *Sedum* 'Autumn Joy', but *Baptisia australis, Physostegia, Rudbeckia, Perilla, Stachys officinalis,* and *Iris sibirica* all add interest through the winter months." In addition, she admires the shiny bronze mats of *Ajuga reptans,* spiky tufts of silver dianthus, and evergreen thymes with foliage colors that range from pale blue-gray to a green that is almost black.

Extraordinary as it may seem, I came across many of these same plants in Lauren Springer's inspiring book, *The Undaunted Garden.* The author gardens in northern Colorado, but the chapter called "The Winter Garden: Myth or Reality" is full of lessons for cold-climate gardeners, wherever they live.

Winter is a serious business on the Keweenaw Peninsula, in northern Michigan. Minimum temperatures there range between minus ten and minus twenty degrees Fahrenheit. "Although we are in the far north," writes my gardening friend Mary Kordes, "we have Lake Superior to moderate our temperatures. She also wallops us with tons of snow." Moisture released by the open water meets the cold Canadian air and produces almost daily snowstorms during January and February.

As Mary describes it, "Our Lake Superior snow has special properties. It has the ability to cling to itself and pile up on everything it falls upon. Snow snakes form on the trees and seem to undulate along the branches, sometimes slipping down and hanging in loops. Mushroom caps form on tree stumps, and as the snowcover on the ground deepens and the stumps are finally lost, the caps just become rounded bumps. A snowshoe walk in the woods is great fun — the snow piles up on trees and shrubs and stumps to form whimsical figures. It's like cloud-gazing on the ground!"

Mary's husband, Dick, carves and whittles his way through the long winter. One year he fashioned a Norwegian bentwood box from their own poplar wood; the design of chair lacing that embellishes it is made from cedar roots gathered from their trees. Another year he mastered the art of weaving Nantucket lightship baskets. Mary wrote that "the wood was from a lovely large oak we lost to wind. Dick also made his own mold over which he wove the baskets. Then he steamed and shaped the handles and rims." Snug and content in the house that Dick built for their retirement, the Kordeses patiently await the renewal of spring.

Not all cold-climate gardeners are as sanguine about northern winters as Mary and Dick Kordes. Sarah Milek, a passionate herb gardener, gets through the season in Vermont with the help of a greenhouse. "It's my light therapy," she admits. "I couldn't survive up here without a greenhouse. I do standards of rosemarys and lavenders and putter about with those all winter. Gary paints in the greenhouse, and along about March, it's sky-blue with rosemary flowers. He paints still lifes of the plants. That's how we rationalize keeping the greenhouse going in this climate." Gary Milek is an artist, and together, he and Sarah run Cider Hill Publications, a cottage industry combining Sarah's knowledge of herbs with his artistic skills. She cultivates flowers and herbs to sell as potpourri and runs the business. He produces fine botanical prints and notecards using her plants as models.

On my first visit to Cider Hill, I remember thinking two things: first, that these people had better own a four-wheel-drive vehicle, and second, that they must be a very self-sufficient pair. Self-sufficiency proved to be the common denominator among all the cold-climate gardeners I met and interviewed. On the whole, they are a tough breed that divides into two camps: those like Mary and Dick, who find winter exhilarating, and those like Sarah, who stoically endure it.

The purpose of this book is to share with you the pleasures of the former and the survival techniques of the latter. It is always intriguing to know what other gardeners are up to, and if their example stirs you to action, so much the better. Whether you garden in the Green, White, or Rocky Mountains, the snowbelt of New York State, or the wilds of Minnesota, you will find inspiration from fellow cold-climate gardeners. There is something for everyone.

A happy few possess the design skills to tackle garden architecture, or "hardscape." Ragna Goddard, who is European by birth, is a graphic designer by profession and a garden-maker by choice and chance. It all began when she and her husband, Tom, also a graphic designer, bought an eighteenth-century farmhouse. "We both got very, very interested in restoring the architecture," she says. "If you were to compare restoration here and in Europe, the focus in this country is primarily on the building. In Europe, you incorporate the landscape as well." The Goddards' gardens are terraced and visually linked with the house. "The gardens here are designed to be beautiful throughout all seasons," says their creator, "because they are architectural gardens."

Just looking out on the garden in winter is not enough for the likes of Joan Larned. Dressed in a warm down jacket, she plunges cheerfully into the cold to prune her orchard trees. Along with her daughter, Avery, she also splits and stacks wood for their maple-sugaring operation. "It's fun," she says. "We have a sugar house that Avery built and woods where we put out five hundred taps. That's why our winters aren't as long as anybody else's."

Other hardy souls employ cold frames and hoop houses to extend the season. Colleen and Gary Allen are natives of Cranberry Island, Maine. From January to March, they are lucky if the mailboat makes it once a day. Isolated from the mainland, they nonetheless manage to continue gardening in a solar-heated greenhouse that they built themselves. Maine is also the adopted state of garden writer Barbara Damrosch and her husband, Eliot Coleman. Eliot's winter exploits are well documented in his book *The Four-Season Harvest,* which describes his method of protecting fall-grown crops for winter harvest. "We think it is so easy to do and so delightful that we're anxious to spread the word," he says. Karen and I are eager to assist them in that endeavor.

If midwinter visits to the cold frame are not your style, what about indoor gardening? Melitta Collier has a plant room where she grows ferns, orchids, African violets, and tropical foliage plants hydroponically. Other determined gardeners bring the outdoors in, employing facilities that run the gamut from windowsills to spare bedrooms to bona fide greenhouses. There are also seed sowers who repair to their basements and garden under lights.

Birds bring life and color to the winter landscape, and one of their champions had a garden designed especially for their benefit. Herb grower Christine Utterback asked Mary Ann McGourty, of Hillside Gardens in Norfolk, Connecticut, to put in a bird garden. Mary Ann obliged with an informal hedge of burning bush, grasses, fruit-laden viburnums, and native hollies.

A whole new world of winter gardening was revealed to me when I visited Pinkie Roe, a professed "flower show jock." The Philadelphia Flower Show, where she is a regular exhibitor, has two major sections. "The horticultural section has all the potted plants, all these wonderful things from people's greenhouses, forced bulbs and things like that," she says. "The arranging section has displays in niches of different sizes. These are lighted boxes, sort of like phone booths. If you are really serious, you have your own practice niches of the correct size so you can mock up your exhibits." Pinkie is serious, and beginning on New Year's Day, her dining room becomes a workroom where she prepares her displays.

While the competitive groom their show entries, the practical mend and sharpen their tools and make things for and from their gardens. Hugh Davis fashions miniature oak gates for the garden and for sale. He uses an antique shave horse set up on the huge hearth in the Davises' eighteenth-century farm kitchen. Rita Buchanan sits in her greenhouse spinning wool she has dyed with plants from her summer garden. And Betsy Williams works with dried plants from her own garden and other sources.

For Betsy, dried herbs and flowers are a way of life. She and a staff of five produce distinctive dried arrangements in a small barn on the Williams property. The ceiling is festooned with dried flowers and myrtle, and the workroom smells delicious. Betsy's advice to would-be flower driers is to try different methods: "If you are interested in drying, you should learn a little bit about the various ways of doing it, including microwave drying. Take, say, five pieces of one kind of plant material. Try it air-dried, try it in the oven, try it in silica gel, sand, and kitty litter." In other words, be adventurous.

Of all the activities that engage gardeners in the winter, none is more popular than getting together with other gardeners. Members of the North American Rock Garden Society flock to their Winter Study Weekend, and small, informal study groups spring up like mushrooms everywhere. Winter is for meeting and sharing. It is also a time for reflection and solitude, for resting and daydreaming. It is the pause that refreshes.

If you have always been one of those gardeners who dread winter, Karen and I hope this book will change your mind about the cold months of the year. It offers ideas for the active and insights for the contemplative. Welcome to the unsung season.

The Unsung Season

Inner Resources

"Inner Resources" might be an alternate title for this book. In both a practical and a figurative sense, the gardeners interviewed are all people who have created their own winter gardening opportunities, indoors and out. Some have reinvented the garden in crafts. Others have prolonged the garden year with season-extending devices. Those in the next few chapters have brought the garden into the house.

Even if you have only a windowsill, you can enjoy the comfort of keeping in touch with growing things during the winter. But for the moment, imagine that you have an untenanted bedroom with a southern exposure. If you can turn off the heat, so much the better. We have just such a bedroom. Because we are surrounded by woodland and our nineteenth-century house has seldom-cleaned, twelve-over-twelve windows, the light quality is far from perfect. To augment the somewhat filtered winter sunshine, my husband has set up lights for my plants.

In front of the south-facing windows we have placed a table made from three two-by-ten-inch pine planks eight feet long supported by a sawhorse at each end. My husband cut the legs of the sawhorses so the table would be the same height as the windowsills. The lights — two double shop lights, with ordinary fluorescent tubes four feet long — are suspended on chains from a sort of gallows above the table. The gallows is made from one-by-three-inch pine. The chains allow me to lower and raise the lights.

With the radiators off, the heat at night sometimes drops as low as forty-eight degrees Fahrenheit. The daytime temperature is about ten degrees warmer, depending on the weather outside. The temperature range is comparable to a cool greenhouse. If it gets up to fifty degrees outside, I shut the door to the rest of the house and open a window. I learned from Tovah Martin, whom you will meet shortly, that indoor plants like a breath of fresh air.

I don't grow many indoor plants for their own sake, but I love being able to carry over plants for the terrace this way. I haul in a beloved fuchsia and take cuttings of *Plectranthus, Brugmansia,* and pelargoniums. I also pot up some rather tender ivies and bring them in. Although indoor decoration is secondary, the bedroom does look attractive in a businesslike way. Besides, there is something special about a plant that you nurture through the winter.

Karen Bussolini does much the same thing, only she has a greenhouse window. Made from old storm sashes and no longer in the first flush of youth, it was already there when she and John bought their house. "The thing was badly designed, badly constructed, and leaks, so we built a frame and put plastic over it to make a kind of interior storm window. But despite its shortcomings, it gives us enormous pleasure," she says.

Located on the southeast side of the house, the greenhouse window gets the first light of morning in addition to the afternoon sun. An apple tree overhangs the window and provides shade in the summer. In the winter, it affords another bonus: "The early morning sun shines through the branches and casts shadows of each twig on the opposite kitchen wall. We can also see the shadows of the birds hopping from twig to twig."

The window is thirty-five inches high and forty-eight inches wide, and the shelf that juts out from it is thirty inches deep. This boxlike structure is covered with a sloping roof attached to the outside of the house two feet higher than the interior opening, so that Karen can grow tall plants at the front of the shelf.

Even before she brings in the bulbs that she pots in the fall and stores in her unheated garden house, the greenhouse window begins to overflow with flowers. Last November she wrote: "My little window is full already, and forced bulbs haven't even entered the picture. Your fuchsia 'Gartenmeister Bonstedt' is blooming its head off. By the way, I've made cuttings of a lovely lime-green plectranthus — would you like one?" (The answer, of course, was affirmative.)

"In the early winter," Karen continued, "I have tender bulbs that you don't have to give much cold treatment, like the paper-whites, and by late winter the amaryllis are coming along. I keep them in cold storage for two months at forty-five to fifty-five degrees. John made me a bulb box with hardware cloth so the mice can't get at anything. I've also got puschkinia, miniature daffodils, and little tulips, and in the spring, after the bulbs are over, I'll start all kinds of seeds."

If simple arrangements like my spare bedroom and Karen's greenhouse window are such an addition to our winter lives, the enthusiasm of gardeners who have plant rooms and greenhouses is understandable.

Melitta Collier

In January 1993, the *American Horticulturist,* a publication of the American Horticultural Society, devoted a whole news issue to cures for the winter blahs. I was intrigued by one of these: hydroponics made easy — and amusing — by Melitta Collier. When an interviewer asked her about some of the procedures recommended by other authorities, she said, "I don't do that. Gardening is supposed to be fun." I thought she sounded like fun and tucked her name away in a file. When the opportunity to write this book arose, I thought of her at once.

Melitta has always been interested in growing plants in containers. Some sixty years ago, when she was in kindergarten, she contracted pneumonia and had to miss school. During her illness, her Sunday school class sent her a potted plant. She remembers the arrival of that gift as clearly as if it were yesterday: "There was a wax begonia and an asparagus fern in a clay pot, and I just thought it was the most beautiful thing I'd ever seen." Her earlier indoor gardening efforts had been confined to sticking plants in old soup cans. This was her first real flowerpot and the beginning of a lifelong affection for houseplants.

Both Melitta's grandmothers were plant lovers, but the urge to grow skipped a generation. "My dad was a carpenter," Melitta says, "and he was always pretty tired by the end of a day. But Dad's father was an outdoor gardener and had a beautiful yard." Her paternal grandparents came from Germany, and she is proud of her heritage. "My grandfather was the Lutheran pastor in Greenvine, Texas. He came to the United States by way of New York and Ellis Island. We had his name put on the wall there."

Melitta's grandfather's parsonage in Greenvine had a huge fig tree that shaded an L-shaped porch. "In the corner of the porch, my grandmother had this enormous Boston fern that I used to sit and look at and drool over." Her grandmother on the other side of the family also grew ferns, which to this day are Melitta's favorite indoor plants. "I like the maidenhairs and the Boston ferns [*Nephrolepis exaltata* 'Bostoniensis']," she says. "Then there are all the sports of the Boston fern. One that I really covet is called 'Irish Lace'. I also love the selaginellas, which are sort of halfway between ferns and mosses." These, along with African violets, begonias, palms, orchids, and tropical foliage plants, flourish in her plant room. And they are all grown hydroponically.

Hydroponics is the practice of growing plants in a solution of water and nutrients, without soil. According to Melitta, "For the houseplant gardener, it is the greatest thing since the invention of the flowerpot." Coming from her, that is high praise. She first became aware of the technique during the Second World War, when the army used hydroculture to produce food for troops stationed on the soilless atolls of the South Pacific. Later the military used the system to grow vegetables in Korea, thus avoiding health risks (local produce was fertilized with "night soil" removed from privies). But it was an article in the *Washington Post* that launched Melitta's career in hydroponics.

She learned about a company called Deco Plants, which sold houseplants and hydroponic supplies at gatherings like Tupperware parties. As an experienced grower, she found the Deco plant selection boring, but she was fascinated by the method. She even worked for Deco for a while. "When I had the parties, I pushed the supplies and the system rather than the plants, which were expensive for what they were," she says. "However, I was completely sold on the technique and did well enough that they didn't tell me to quit." Melitta quickly tired of the Monday night meetings, though. One regular feature of them was for the Deco representatives to march around the room singing the company song. "That's what did it for me!" she says with a laugh.

Although it was fall when I visited Melitta in Silver Spring, Maryland, the weather was still warm enough for the houseplants to be outside. We shared their lath enclosure at lunchtime. Her husband, Bill, joined us for a delicious meal reflecting Melitta's interest in Vietnamese cooking. She became enamored of the cuisine when she and Bill lived in Saigon, where Bill worked for the U.S. government for several years.

After lunch, Melitta and I talked hydroponics in the plant room, which has skylights and windows that face southeast and southwest. "In the winter, when the trees are bare and the sun is low in the sky, I get a lot of sun — not so much through the skylights but through the windows," she says. Formerly an open patio, the plant room was enclosed by Bill the year he retired. A friend who was an electrical engineer ran gas and water lines to the new room and did the wiring.

A fan runs winter and summer to provide air circulation, and heat is supplied in cold weather by a gas heater. Winter temperatures range from fifty-eight to sixty degrees, unless Melitta is out there for any length of time, in which case she gives herself a bit of extra heat for comfort. The plant room boasts a small pool, a fountain, and a resident toad. "I discovered the toad one year after it had become real cold," she explains. "I thought, 'I can't put him outside now.' So he stayed and has seemed fat and sassy ever since. Once in a while I go out and buy some mealworms and give him a treat." Although the toad often vanishes for weeks at a time, Melitta's grandchildren can always find him.

In this relaxed, homey atmosphere, with the sound of the fountain in the background, Melitta began to talk about her experience in growing houseplants without soil. "I think hydroponics is a wonderful technique," she says. "I don't even like soil at all anymore. It's a dirty four-letter word. I try to keep my yard looking decent, but I have arthritis and am becoming more and more limited as to how much outdoor gardening I can do. Indoor plants you can do year-round. It is never more glorious in here than when the snow is flying outside."

She has been growing hydroponically for twenty-five years and spreads the word by giving garden-club lectures and workshops. It is a disappointment to her that so far the technique has been slow to catch on. She attributes part of the problem to the available books on the subject. "Most books on hydroponics are about growing vegetables and herbs," she says. "They show you these ridiculous homemade hydroculture systems that always involve a bucket and a hose that you run water through two or three times a day. These things would look terrible on a coffee table. I grow decorative plants. I'm not interested in crops."

She uses instead a simple system of manmade clay pebbles in plastic pots with water-level indicators. The kiln-fired clay pebbles replace soil for anchorage and moisture storage. They have a neutral pH and are very porous; the plant draws up water by capillary action and the pebbles hold it in reserve until the plant needs it. Air spaces between the pebbles provide ample oxygen for roots. Water-level indicators and pebbles are available by mail from a number of companies that specialize in hydroponic supplies.

For a beginner, the easiest thing to do is to invest in a couple of containers designed specifically for hydroculture. These have an outer, decorative pot and an inner, "culture" pot. The plant is placed in the inner pot, which has perforated sides. A built-in gauge measures the water level in the outer pot. You can't go wrong, because you water only when a visible float sinks to the bottom of the gauge.

According to Melitta, any watertight container can be used to grow plants hydroponically, but a water gauge is "absolutely essential." If you use your own container, choose one with no holes, fill it with the proper stones, and add water to a level not more than one third the height of the container. The water level is critical — never more than a third the height of the pot. The plant roots grow in and among the stones, not in the reservoir of water. However, they frequently work their way down to water level. When they do, Melitta removes these lower roots: "I keep them cut off because you want to encourage feeder roots nearer the plant."

Compared to growing plants in potting soil, she claims, hydroculture is "a breeze." The stones are clean, lightweight, and odor-free. They last indefinitely and can be washed and reused. They provide constant, even moisture but never get soggy, and you never have to worry about over- or underwatering, because "anyone can look at a water gauge and tell whether water is needed." Fertilizing is just as easy. Although you can use diluted liquid plant food, Melitta has switched to a granular time-release fertilizer, which she sprinkles over the stones every four to six months.

The technique of growing plants hydroponically has been around for a long time. It is thought that the Hanging Gardens of Babylon were based on a primitive form of hydroponics. Rice has always been grown hydroponically, and modern installations provide a variety of vegetables for desert countries such as Israel, Lebanon, and Kuwait. Today the technique also enjoys great popularity in Europe. When the Colliers were in Germany recently, all the plants they saw in hotels, banks, and restaurants were grown hydroponically. "In Berlin there is a famous shopping mall with big, big planters — all done with the same stones I use," says Melitta.

She herself has installed large-scale hydroponic plantings at the Lutheran Church of St. Andrew in Wheaton, Maryland. When an addition to the church was built, Melitta talked the interior decoration committee into trying hydroculture in their new planters. Just inside the main entrance, on either side of the doors, are four rectangular troughs filled with tall cane begonias, bamboo palms, fishtail palms, fiddle-leaf figs, Chinese evergreens, dracaenas, and rex begonias with spectacular silver-and-purple leaves.

"Because the light is not all that it should be for plants that bloom, I've tried to make it interesting with variegated and textured foliage," she says. "At Christmas I set in pots of red and white poinsettias, and for Easter, hydrangeas and lilies. These additions are left in their pots of soil."

Melitta and her daughter check water levels in the hydroponic planters once a week and fertilize them every few months. Otherwise the plants receive no care whatever and reward this neglect with a splendid display of handsome foliage.

Plants that begin life with their roots in soil have to be introduced to hydroculture. Melitta explains what you have to do: "First, clean the roots — you have to get all the soil off. Use a strong jet of water and comb through the roots with your fingers. It's important to remove *all* the soil, because any that's left behind will decompose and can cause rot." She often treats the plants being conditioned as if they were cuttings. The cleaned plants are set into moist Perlite in an aquarium covered with a sheet of glass to keep in the humidity. In the moist environment, they soon develop new roots.

Melitta took me into a rather untidy workroom where many small African violet plants were rooting under lights. There were pots and containers everywhere. "This is my chamber of horrors," she said cheerfully. "Every time somebody comes, Bill says, 'Don't let them in there!' But I want to show you what I do with African violets. They love hydroculture." She took a small plant out of the aquarium, shook most of the Perlite off its roots, and planted it in clay pebbles, just as you would in soil. Perlite, unlike soil, does not break down. If a little still clings to the roots, it doesn't matter, because it won't decompose.

For a time Melitta toyed with the idea of writing a book about growing ornamental plants hydroponically, but she decided against it. "Once you know the system and the technique of getting plants into hydroculture, what's to write about?" she says. "The important thing is to know your plants. That's the part you need to learn. You have to know what you are growing and how they want to be grown — their light, humidity, and temperature requirements. You need to know what insects to watch out for, and how to groom your plants and keep them clean."

I think Melitta should write that book after all.

Sarah and Gary Milek

Winter comes to southeastern Vermont in fits and starts. Usually there is a night or two of killing frost in the beginning of September, which wipes out Sarah Milek's basil and zinnias. "After that," she says, "we have a marvelous warm October, and November is a gorgeous month. It's cold, but we usually don't have snow, and you have beautiful, subtle colors in the countryside around you. It's a very special time of year. Gary loves it for painting, because the skies are wonderful."

While Sarah enjoys the fall, winter is not her favorite season. "We expect a two-week period somewhere toward the end of January when we have temperatures of twenty-eight below zero. Then we have a February thaw, which is heavenly, and you think, 'Oh my God, this is fabulous. We've gotten through winter. The days are getting longer, we're getting more light, and it's absolutely wonderful.' But of course winter is *far* from over."

Nevertheless, having a greenhouse makes life in the frozen north tolerable. The Mileks have had their hoop greenhouse for twelve years, but it looks like new because the plastic shell has recently been replaced. Heat is provided by a large oil burner in the cellar of their house, which pumps hot water to the greenhouse, where it circulates through a system of pipes. Warm air is dispersed by a fan and a heat exchanger.

The size, thirty-two feet by twenty-seven feet, is perfect for the Mileks' purposes. Sarah does topiaries of rosemary and lavender, and she and Gary raise annuals, vegetables, herbs, and perennials for their gardens. The gardens in turn furnish Gary with models for his paintings and Sarah with flowers and foliage for her potpourris.

Gary modified the original design of the greenhouse by closing in both ends with solid, well-insulated walls. There are pressure-treated sills, and the earth floor is covered with trap rock. The structure has no footings. Instead, the metal hoops that support the plastic cover lock onto pipes driven deep into the ground. A giant fig tree growing out of the floor has reached the ceiling and has to be kept in check by pruning.

Except for the fig tree, the greenhouse is free of plants during the summer, but in the winter it is crammed with rosemary (*Rosmarinus officinalis*), lavender (*Lavandula officinalis*), African mallow (*Anisodontea hypomandarum*), and florist's broom (*Genista canariensis*), as well as dozens of different scented geraniums, bay trees (*Laurus nobilis*), and ivies (*Hedera helix*).

Gary moves into his winter quarters in October, after the first frost. Every fall he does a series of greenhouse paintings, arranging vegetables and herbs from the outdoor garden as still lifes. In the winter he paints groups of potted herbs and portraits of individual plants.

By March, the rosemarys are covered with tiny pale blue flowers. Sarah describes herself as "dedicated to rosemary" and plans to write a descriptive booklet about this fascinating herb. She grows hundreds of small rosemary plants and starts training them. Large topiaries require years of careful pruning and are expensive, but she can sell the small plants at a reasonable price at the topiary workshops she gives.

With the arrival of summer, Gary returns to his studio in the house that he designed and built. From the outside, the house looks like a Cape with an extension at the back. The kitchen, dining room, and living room, which make up the extension, are all open to one another and have many windows overlooking the Connecticut River Valley.

The view is beautiful. The land sweeps down toward the town of Windsor, rising again in a ridge of blueberry-blue hills across the river in New Hampshire. A staircase in the east wing of the house leads down to the office of Cider Hill Publications, the business that makes it possible for the Mileks to live and garden on this remote New England hilltop.

At the foot of their knoll, a second entrance to the property gives access to a small barn, where Sarah and Gary lived while they were building the main house. This structure now accommodates the frame shop. In addition to cards reproduced from Gary's original watercolor paintings, Cider Hill Publications offers prints in limited editions, complete with fine wood frames made on the premises. The frame shop's former incarnation was the cider mill that gave the Mileks' cottage industry its name.

When they bought the land in 1974, it was a jungle of old apple trees swathed in wild shrubs, vines, and blackberry canes. To their surprise, the trees bore a bountiful harvest of fruit, and the young couple felt obliged to do something with it. When they came across an old cider press, their fate was clear. In 1977 they began producing cider. However, Cider Hill was too far off the beaten track, and Sarah had to look for a more accessible sales outlet. Fifteen miles farther north, in the town of Norwich, she found a farmers' market. Cider sold so briskly there that the Mileks were inspired to think up other ways of making their land work for them. Sarah began selling homemade jams and jellies. Fresh herbs and vegetables came next, and finally flowers — fresh-cut flowers at first, then dried flowers.

So successful was Sarah at creating original arrangements of her own dried flowers that suddenly the Mileks were swamped. "I got into dried flowers just on the crest of the wave. It was really coming through this country like mad in the early eighties," she says. "At that time, we were growing more than a hundred different kinds of flowers for drying, like helichrysums, statices, and everlastings, every year." Before long she was supplying Windsor House Vermont State Craft Center with bouquets, tussie-mussies, wreaths, and arrangements. The work was a joy. Experimenting with color, form, and texture gave Sarah enormous pleasure.

But success was nearly the undoing of the Mileks. In 1984 a glowing magazine article drew attention to the heretofore secret world of Cider Hill.

"It was a disastrous affair for us," says Gary. "People from all over the world began coming up the driveway and out of the woods to see how we did everything — why our life was so happy and pleasurable — and it was awful. It stopped the dried flower business." Sarah explained that there was more to it than the shock of having their privacy invaded. She found herself managing a staff of helpers instead of doing what she had been doing herself with real enjoyment. "I wasn't having a very good time trying to get other people to make things the way I made them. That's how the print business came about. One day we sat down at the round table in the kitchen and bounced around ideas." The result of that brainstorming session was Cider Hill Publications.

The impetus for the new venture was a garden-club talk Sarah had given. Because she had no slides to illustrate the plants that were her subject, she asked Gary to do some illustrations. "He just threw together these sketches for me, and afterwards people came up to me and said, 'The talk was lovely, and by the way, are the pictures for sale, can we have these?' So we decided we would produce prints — always keeping it to herbs and flowers. I took on managing the business and am the product development department."

Besides prints, notecards, and greeting cards of Gary's work, Cider Hill Publications offers Sarah's own blend of potpourri and two symbolic herbal mixes, one for weddings and one for the blessing of a new home. As much as possible, the Mileks grow the roses, perennials, and herbs that contribute petals and foliage to these products. The wedding mix contains everlastings (for obvious reasons), lavender for luck, mints for hospitality, thyme and rosemary for remembrance, and sage for domestic virtue. "We grow the sage, thyme, and some of the lavender," Sarah explains.

At least three times a year the Mileks drag themselves away from their hilltop to set up displays at gift and stationery shows. These events run for several days at a time and are exhausting, but returning home soon restores the Mileks' equilibrium. "If we're able to have a couple of days in the garden after we get back, it puts life together in the right way again," says Sarah.

When I first called to ask Sarah about participating in this book, I asked

The author pots up snowdrops for indoor decoration.

The first snowdrops (*Galanthus nivalis*) push through snow in the author's garden.

Witch hazel (*Hamamelis* x *intermedia* 'Sunburst') blooms in February.

In February, Karen Bussolini's window greenhouse is
filled with forced narcissus, plectranthus cuttings, ivies,
and a standard fuschia 'Gartenmeister Bonstedt'.

Daffodil and tulip bulbs for
forcing lie among Karen's
potting supplies.

Joy Martin watches her daughter-in-law Tovah shape a spherical topiary in one of Logee's greenhouses.

Gary Milek makes sketches for a painting in the greenhouse, his winter studio. By February he is surrounded by clouds of rosemary flowers and pink Siberian wallflowers.

Opposite: The collection of plants in this corner of Melitta Collier's plant room, formerly an outdoor patio, includes Boston fern and some tropical plants growing in an automated hydroponic planter under lights.

A bed of *Ilex decidua,* commonly called possum haw, adds color to the winter landscape at Barnard's Inn Farm.

Polly Hill's arbor of hornbeam (*Carpinus betulus* 'Columnaris') is woven and pruned into a lacy tunnel.

Joanna Reed's terrace garden is furnished with silver-gray lamb's ears, pewter-colored lavenders, and blue-green *Euphorbia myrsinites*. A pale yellow witch hazel in full bloom rises above this rich carpet of subtle colors.

Dried stalks and flower heads of sedum are still eye-catching in early March.

if her husband was equally passionate about gardening. "Oh God, yes!" she replied. "I think he goes to bed with a plant catalogue every single night of the year." The fruits of their joint labors are in evidence everywhere. At the back of the house, long rectangular perennial beds run parallel to each other. When I was there in late August, the shrub roses were beginning to rebloom and there were masses of phlox, rudbeckia, globe thistle, pink-flowered burnet (*Sanguisorba obtusa*), and late-flowering daylilies. The Mileks love daylilies and collect cultivars named for painters.

Between these beds and the house lies a large island garden, wet on one side and dry on the other. A big patch of bee balm was blooming on the dry side, and I could see strapping rosettes of Japanese primrose (*Primula japonica*) foliage in the wet area. On the west side of the house, raised beds contain culinary and scented herbs, and for the time being, a big square plot serves as a vegetable, herb, and cutting garden. But Sarah has other plans. Her winter project is to redesign that space as a formal herb garden.

Idyllic as life in this beautiful setting appears, the Mileks have a strenuous work week. Part-time helpers begin arriving at the office beneath Gary's studio at eight-thirty in the morning, and Sarah works until at least five every day doing the managing, marketing, and shipping. Then there is the huge push to prepare for the trade shows. Nor has the road to their hilltop been direct or easy.

At the time they met, the Mileks had both been married before, and between them they had five young children. Sarah's were then five and eight; Gary's, aged five, nine, and twelve. "In fact, that's how we met," he told me. "She had a nursery school in Walpole, New Hampshire." Sarah laughed and said they were destined to meet anyway. She was already familiar with Gary's paintings and was curious about the artist who painted gardens. A mutual friend, also an artist, introduced them, and Gary began bringing his children to Sarah's day-care center.

The house was built with this menage in mind, and in the early years everything the Mileks did was a family affair — market garden, beehives, cider mill, and chickens. The chickens became too much work for too little return, but Sarah misses them. She says, "I'm yearning for a few chickens, and now there is a system where you have a tiny little chicken house and a long narrow run for them. It's portable, so you can put it in the garden and move it from row to row so the chickens actually weed your garden and fertilize it. I would love to do that, but we would have to figure out how to winter the chickens over."

Sarah's love of rural life is in part a result of her years at the Putney School in Vermont. "For me," she says, "it was the perfect solution to a miserable situation, which was that I had to go away to school. Most boarding schools were so claustrophobic and structured — indoors and uniforms. It didn't work for me. Then it just happened that my family moved to South America for a few years, so instead of completing Putney, I did my senior year down in Chile. I didn't go to college." Instead, she went to the School of the Boston Museum of Fine Arts and the New School for Social Research, in New York City, where she studied painting. "The gardens," she says, "are an extension of all that."

Gary began with gardens. "My father grew strawberries in Manchester, Connecticut. He had thirty acres of strawberries, so I have always had my hands in the ground." But as a child he also studied art, at the Wadsworth Athenaeum, in nearby Hartford. While these two parallel threads have been constants in his life, at college, art took a back seat to sports. Having received scholarships in art and soccer at Syracuse University, he found himself torn between the two. The soccer team was on the road for four or five days a week, and he dropped behind with his work in art and received a painful jolt when his painting instructor failed him for late work. He acknowledges now that it was a good thing, because it forced him to review his priorities. Art won, and he dropped soccer. Laughing, he admits that Syracuse was a football college and had a lousy soccer team anyway.

I feel half guilty, prying life stories from modest, quiet people like the Mileks, but there is always so much to learn. One thing I've found out is that gardeners are happier than most people, and happy people are like magnets. They attract those who wish to learn their recipe for contentment and satisfaction. Despite the hard work that supports their lifestyle, Sarah and Gary Milek are happy.

They disclaim any special secret or credit. "When you like what you are doing," says Gary, "you don't think of it as work. You just think of it as your way of life. That's important. We start in the morning when the light comes up and go to bed when the chores are finished — that's our day."

Logee's Greenhouses

For gardeners all over the United States, Logee's is the supreme inner resource. In winter, the "fond and wayward thoughts" that slide into a gardener's head are of the greenhouses in Danielson, Connecticut — sweet thoughts of fragrant Carolina jasmine (*Gelsemium sempervirens*), perfumed gardenias, and delicious lemon-scented honeybells (*Hermannia verticillata*), and wicked thoughts about buying one of every single scented-leaf geranium in Logee's Herb House: 'Apricot', 'Attar of Roses', 'Chocolate Peppermint', 'Cinnamon', 'Coconut', 'Ginger', 'Lemon Balm', 'Lime', 'Nutmeg', 'Orange', and 'Strawberry'.

Plants from every corner of the world fill an aggregation of greenhouses. In the Long House, benches crowded with hundreds of small pots line the outside walls on either side. A wide raised bed filled with soil runs down the middle. This is where the stock plants are grown. Some of them are huge and old. The paths separating the benches from the stock bed are so narrow that you have to squeeze sideways to let another person pass.

The Long House is kept relatively cool, and this is where you will find abutilons, known a century ago as parlor maples for their sharply lobed foliage. Because the tissue-paper flowers come in mouthwatering shades of coral pink, butter yellow, tangerine, old rose, and Valentine red, you feel that you have to have one of each. Catering to this unbridled urge, Logee's offers a collection of five for a special price. Who could be without that?

If you are susceptible to gorgeous foliage, steer clear of the begonias. They are a specialty of the house. Byron Martin, grandson of the founder, William D. Logee, hybridizes begonias and received an award from the American Begonia Society for his introduction 'Midnight Sun'. This cultivar is described in the catalogue as having "center leaves of translucent pink with green veins and rosy red underneath, with the outer leaves of moss green." If you think that sounds dangerous, try a rex begonia called 'Firmament': "This glowing hybrid has leaves of all shades of pink to silver set against bronze, like the evening sunset."

Gardeners from every state and from other countries make pilgrimages to Logee's. Those who can't undertake the journey to the small Connecticut town find vicarious thrills in the mail-order catalogue. This slender, glossy publication has excellent color photographs by another Logee grandson, Geoffrey Martin, and his wife, the garden writer Tovah Martin. Tovah is also responsible for the alluring plant descriptions that make the catalogue so hard for homebound gardeners to resist.

The phenomenal success of this small family-owned business can be explained in part by a paragraph from the letter that accompanied its hundredth anniversary catalogue. The tone is as warm, friendly, and down-home as the plant offerings are rare, exotic, and extensive: "A century ago, Grandpa Logee first opened shop on North Street, selling flowers and plants from his small glass house. That original greenhouse is still standing (along with several newer additions), and the Logee family continues to own and operate the business. We do our own growing and propagating; we write, design, and photograph the catalogue. And we send plants throughout the country and the world. We send double daturas and fragrant jasmines to gardeners in little towns, we send rex begonias and passionflowers to huge botanical gardens."

A strong, flexible web of family relationships has sustained Logee's Greenhouses for more than a hundred years and will no doubt carry the business triumphantly into the twenty-first century. At the present time, a multigenerational quartet runs the show: Joy Logee Martin, matriarch of the clan; her brother, Richard Logee; her son Byron; and her daughter-in-law Tovah.

On the day of my interview with Joy and Tovah, a large plant order was being assembled for shipment to the Middle East. Tovah, a tiny, intensely alive woman, met me in the little sales lobby, where we perched on a bench until Joy arrived. Meanwhile, a steady stream of customers wandered in and out and the phone never stopped ringing. Serene in the midst of the confusion, Joy Martin joined us, and for the next hour the three of us moved from place to place, trying to find a quiet spot. We settled finally in the packing room, where workmen were mending the roof. In a greenhouse, maintenance is an ongoing winter chore.

As Logee's is the ultimate resource for gardeners in winter, I asked Joy and Tovah to suggest plants suitable for typical indoor situations. Tovah led off with windowsills, a subject dear to her heart and one about which she has recently written a splendid book called *Well-Clad Windowsills*. "It seems to me there's so much you can do creatively with a windowsill," she explains. "It's an undiscovered frontier, because we don't really do that much with design on the windowsill. Often people just line up their plants in soldier-straight rows on their little plant shelves. It is as if the windowsill never moved further forward than an annual garden of the forties and fifties, when everything was planted in a nice straight line. Since then we've moved more toward the English aesthetic of mixed borders. We should do the same with windowsill gardening. We should think about design, form, and color combinations. You might want something sprawling and something upright, something that looks like a tree, and something that cascades down, just as you would in the garden."

In choosing plants for your windowsills, you must remember the importance of light. In her new book Tovah tells readers how to choose the right plants for the right exposure. Sunny south-facing windows are a boon if you fall for abutilons or love geraniums. East windows with strong morning light are good for clivias, African violets, and the closely related Cape primroses

(*Streptocarpus*). If you have a west window, there is the whole world of begonias. For a northern exposure, Tovah says, forget flowers, but as long as the window is unobstructed, ferns and ivy will thrive.

Temperature is less critical to successful indoor gardening than light, she says. "People panic too much about temperatures. Plants really prefer what is considered a little chilly for a home environment — except for the real, real tropicals, like the begonias and the African violet family." Joy adds a word of caution here: "If your night temperature is above sixty, then you can grow the tropicals. But if your heat goes down to fifty, you would have to use herbs and other cold-tolerant plants."

In recent years, interest in heat conservation has made plants that can take a nighttime temperature of fifty degrees popular. Suggestions were offered as an antiphonal chant. Tovah: "Jasmines do very well in cool temperatures — *Jasminum polyanthum,* especially. It's winter-flowering and usually blooms for Valentine's Day." Joy: "Camellias — they like it cool. We have twenty-five varieties, at least, and they're winter-blooming, of course. They flower from Thanksgiving to Easter. Fuchsias love cool temperatures. There's one in particular that I highly recommend, and it flowers year-round — *Fuchsia* 'Honeysuckle'. It's a beautiful thing. It grows flowers from the tip of each branch." Tovah: "And old roses. Even *Rosa* 'Cecile Brunner' does very well indoors. Roses only perform when it's cool. 'Cecile Brunner' flowers in late February and into March. It's really divine." And so the afternoon went: plants and ideas, first from one, then from the other.

When the subject of watering came up, Joy said, "Let me tell you a little story. When Byron was in kindergarten, he had charge of the plants in the schoolroom. On Monday morning, Miss Leach said, 'Byron, have you checked the plants today?' He jumped up and ran to the pots and felt the soil. He had seen his mother feel the soil and then water. He said, 'Not today, Miss Leach.' When the surface of the soil is dry, water and water thoroughly. Then wait for it to dry out again. That's a good rule for most plants."

The Logee family is a rarity. As the twentieth century draws to an end, it is unusual to find adults still living in their hometown, let alone living and working where their parents and their grandparents lived and worked before them. Bound by the ties of blood, mutual respect, and affection and a shared devotion to plants, the Logees have prospered on a plot of land that once belonged to Joy's great-grandfather.

A visit to the Logee homestead nearby is enlightening. Built in 1896 by William D. Logee, the house is filled with memories and memorabilia. The front parlor, used only for state occasions, looks exactly as it did when Joy's parents were alive, with lace curtains, dark woodwork, and tufted velvet furniture. There are jardinières containing foliage plants, and flower paintings adorn the walls. Rugs and upholstery bloom extravagantly in silk and wool thread.

The back parlor and dining room are where the family lives today. Here the past rubs shoulders with the present. Tovah's Wardian case stands in the tall bay window. Invented by a nineteenth-century British surgeon named Nathaniel Ward, the case resembles a miniature glasshouse supported on elegantly turned cabriole legs. Condensation supplies adequate moisture for plants enclosed in the airtight case, which eliminates the need for watering. Tovah's was built for her by a friend and is an "absolutely, religiously authentic reproduction." The case was designed to hold ferns, which are still the best choice.

In the library, along with a player piano and glass-fronted bookcases, there are dozens of family photos: evocative nineteenth-century group pictures, posed studio portraits, and recent snapshots of grandchildren. The house bears witness to a living, ongoing history. It is this balance of old and new, permanence and change that gives the family its strength and the business its viability. The theme is carried out in Logee's catalogue as well. Heirloom houseplants from Grandpa Logee's original collection are listed alongside the newest of the new hybrids.

The family love of plants can be traced back even further than Joy's father, to a young shoemaker from Ireland, John Mahrs, who emigrated to the United States in the mid-nineteenth century and set up shop in Danielson. He built a house for his family on North Street and, for his own pleasure, a little freestanding greenhouse. In November 1994, I stood in that same greenhouse with his great-granddaughter, admiring a huge ponderosa lemon tree planted by his grandson, Joy's father. "John Mahrs was really my step-great-grandfather," she explained. "My father's mother passed away when he was only four years old, and my grandfather remarried Susan Mahrs. She was the only grandmother I ever knew. Her father had this little hobby greenhouse."

The small wood and glass structure has long since been incorporated into the larger complex of more modern greenhouses, but the ponderosa lemon tree growing out of its earthen floor remains an enduring link with the past. Every year hundreds of cuttings are propagated from this long-lived giant. When I visited, in the fall, the branches were laden with grapefruit-size lemons. "You couldn't have come at a nicer time," said Joy with satisfaction. "It's quite a show right now." Indeed, the display of fruits, each weighing as much as three pounds, was nothing short of spectacular.

The only family member unmoved by plants during the Logees' long association with horticulture seems to have been Joy's grandfather. Nevertheless, he was supportive when his son showed a strong bent in that direction and helped him acquire a suitable education. "When my father was in his teens, there wasn't any such thing as a college where they taught horticulture. So my grandfather found a place in Boston called the J. J. Montgomery Rose Conservatory and got my father a job there," Joy explained. "Later my dad discovered that Grandpa had paid the people at the conservatory a dollar a day to let him work there. And all along, he thought he was actually earning money! Anyway, roses were his first love, and that's what he grew when he had his own greenhouse."

The tenth of fifteen children, Joy remembers selling flowers door-to-door when she was a little girl. "I was about six," she recalls, "and every Sunday after church I used to go up and down the street with bunches of violets. I loved it. I like people so much and am outgoing, so it just comes naturally. My father and brothers, and now my son, who is the manager, recognized a good saleslady when they saw one." By the time she was fourteen, Joy was an indispensable member of the Logee team. She still is.

Five siblings threw in their lot with horticulture and the family business. Ernest, her eldest brother, joined their father in 1922 and was the family's prop and stay until his death. Brother Roger was with them until his marriage; then he and his wife started the Country Greenhouses, a thriving retail flower shop also in Danielson. Another brother, Archie, is a retail florist in Rhode Island. And Richard has remained with the business throughout his career. One sister, who now lives in Maine, was bitten with the plant bug and operates Mary Gardens, in Camden. Fortunately for Logee's Greenhouses, Joy stayed at home and eventually found a kindred spirit in Ernest Evans Martin. "I waited a long time to meet my husband," she says. "He was interested in plants and had always wanted to know about horticulture. Together we built the mail-order business. He was a wonderful grower. He had ten green fingers."

In 1971, Joy's husband died. "It was a very difficult time for all of us," she says simply. But a few months later Tovah turned up, bringing with her youth, energy, and a tremendous excitement about plants. Her presence was like a tonic, and Joy was grateful. "Her arrival was the saving grace for my son Geoffrey, who was in really deep mourning. Tovah pulled him out of it. Then she married into the family."

Unlike the other members of the Logee family, Tovah was not brought up around plants. But she has vivid memories of going to Longwood Gardens, in Kennett Square, Pennsylvania, as a small child. "One of my earliest childhood memories is that one of the gardeners there came over to me — I was tiny — and said, 'Look at that. Those are baby's tears, just like what you cry.' And I remember picking up on that right away. I was very young — right out of the stroller, I think. I've often thought since what a nice man he was, to give me that memory that has lasted throughout my life."

At the age of six, Tovah tackled ivy. "It wasn't something to keep you on the edge of your seat or anything, but it was green and growing. And it started me off," she explains. Later she planted marigolds and harvested the seed as part of a Brownie project, but it wasn't until she was in high school that she discovered herbs. "Right before I went to Antioch College, I became interested in herbs. And while I was there, I became *very* interested. I wanted to pursue their uses and the whole medicinal idea. The thought that plants could be useful fascinated me. Then I came here." Joy finished the story: "She came here on a work-study program and never went back."

There is an old adage that two grown women cannot live under the same roof unless one "bends the knee." Joy and her daughter-in-law have occupied the family house for the past twenty years, and I could detect no knee-bending on either side, only give-and-take and genuine warmth of feeling.

Planted for Winter

For gardeners who train their gaze outward in the winter, there are many wonderful hardy plants to enjoy from the windows. Conifers have arresting shapes and subtle colors. Junipers, firs, spruces, and members of the *Chamaecyparis* tribe offer foliage in shades of gold and blue, purple and bronze. Needled evergreens can be spiky or soft; stiff needles catch tufts of snow, while pliant foliage droops beneath its weight and gives a different effect.

Broadleaf evergreens offer variety in size, leaf shape, and color. Mountain laurel (*Kalmia latifolia*) has elliptical dark-green leaves, and several species of *Leucothoe* boast polished leaves the color of morocco leather or mahogany.

Deciduous trees have much to contribute in pattern, outline, and bark texture. I love bare trees, especially sycamores, with their mottled hides. Just down our road, an enormous specimen presides in pallid splendor over the front yard of a renovated nineteenth-century schoolhouse. The base of this huge tree is brown and scaly, but as the trunk rises toward the crown, the bark fades to bone white beneath patches of taupe, gray, and olive green. The patches peel off in thin flakes, as irregularly regular as the pieces of a jigsaw puzzle.

Though the sycamore is too large for most gardens, other trees have decorative bark and beautiful silhouettes. Everyone admires white birches (*Betula papyrifera*), but river birches (*Betula nigra*) are lovely too, with their shaggy, sunset-orange bark.

Certain shrubs come into focus better without their foliage. The deciduous hollies are eye-catching only when the black twigs are crowded with red fruits and the leaves have fallen. Berried shrubs abound. But I am stealing the thunder of the two amazing gardeners whom you are about to meet. Suffice it to say that in the winter landscape, woody plants reign supreme. Age and the season become them.

A young gardener with the energy, desire, and know-how — and enough room — can grow and get to know a very large number of perennials in a few years. Even the notoriously slow-growing gas plant (*Dictamnus albus*) shows its medals by the age of five. But it takes time for trees and shrubs to prove their worth, and full-grown specimens are one of the perks enjoyed by older gardeners. Between them, Polly Hill and Joanna Reed have been gardening for well over a century. They can introduce you to new and unusual woody treasures for the winter garden.

Polly Hill

Polly Hill's entire property is a winter garden of trees and shrubs. In 1958 she started an arboretum from seed at her summer home, Barnard's Inn Farm, on Martha's Vineyard. She prepared a small nursery bed for her seedlings and enclosed it with chicken wire. Today, tiny plants that once needed protection from rabbits are mature specimens. The open fields that were once divided from one another only by stone walls are now framed with stands of pine, fir, holly, stewartia, and magnolia.

At the entrance to the arboretum, a stately *Magnolia grandiflora* rises higher than the roof of the outbuildings that shelter it from the wind. A southern species, started from seed, this tree took four or five years to learn not to shed its foliage in the winter. But its roots have long since become well established in the rich soil of an old chicken yard, and the large, gleaming evergreen leaves add an unlikely tropical touch to the winter landscape.

As a grower and selector of superior garden subjects, Polly has introduced eighty-two varieties of woody plants — kousa dogwoods, stewartias, hollies, magnolias, rhododendrons, and azaleas, all with winter beauty. The winter attractions of both the Asian dogwoods and the stewartias include bark patterned in brown, tan, and gray. Christmas cards exploit the charms of the spiny-leaved hollies. The magnolias have smooth gray bark and velvet-textured buds, and the foliage of many evergreen azaleas turns a reddish bronze.

Although I was familiar with the Hill azaleas, I had not thought of Polly in connection with winter gardens until I read an essay she wrote for the Brooklyn Botanic Garden's Plants and Gardens series. The essay begins: "My garden at Barnard's Inn Farm on Martha's Vineyard lies in deep repose. It breathes softly, imperceptibly. The shimmering flowers of summer, the riotous leaves of autumn, are gone. What remains are the strong, enduring, sheltering, and quiet forms of trunks and branches." In a few words, she captures the distinctive nature of the unsung season.

In the essay, Polly leads the reader on a winter walk around her property, pointing out the sights she particularly enjoys. She likes the orderly branching of the bald cypress (*Taxodium distichum*) and the angularity of the tulip poplar (*Liriodendron tulipifera*). She draws attention to surface details, like the "rough brown curls" peeling from a paperbark maple (*Acer griseum*), and introduces you to the Vineyard's unique stone walls. Built of rounded boulders in a single course, they are honeycombed with see-through openings. She describes the walls as "lacy" and their color as "greenish, yellowish, or dull orange with lichens."

When I visited, these walls were one of the first things that caught my eye. They are different from Connecticut's massive elephant-gray walls, which are formed by many thicknesses of rock. Vineyard walls have a lightness to them that is very attractive.

My admiration was obvious. "Aren't they marvelous?" said Polly. "I love every one. Locally, the rocks are called glacial pebbles, no matter what size they are — except for really huge individual rocks called glacial erratics. I have one back in the woods that children love to climb on."

I had crossed that morning on the ten-thirty ferry, and despite my protests, Polly insisted on driving the seven miles to meet me. For her, the day had already been busy. She had conducted a houseguest on a whirlwind tour of the farm in her electric grounds cart. Having discharged that responsibility, she had hurried off to collect me. Four hours later, we were back at the ferry slip. In between we had flown over the fields in the yellow cart, trying to fit it all in: the collections of stewartias, camellias, and azaleas, the wonderful arbor of hornbeam, and the beetlebung trees, pruned from the bottom up to form a floating hedge.

I was charmed by the local name "beetlebung" for the pepperidge tree (*Nyssa sylvatica*) and impressed by the way in which the trees had been used. "There are twenty of them in a row," Polly explained. "I'm trying to do what they did down at Dumbarton Oaks — that wonderful circular hedge on stilts. It's too expensive to keep up properly. But mine has had a little of that attention. You can walk along and have the shade of them above you and also enjoy looking out. It makes a good structural effect in the winter, too."

For color in the winter, Polly appreciates the conifers. The seasonal hue of the island landscape is predominantly gray. Shingled buildings like those at Barnard's Inn Farm darken to a black-gray in the salt air. They stand out against fawn-gray fields, which in turn are wrapped in the gray embrace of the surrounding deciduous woodland. Against this muted backdrop, the deep green firs give stellar performances.

The Caucasian fir (*Abies nordmanniana*) "is a wonderful plant — such a rich green." Polly likes the Spanish fir (*Abies pinsapo*), with short, stiff, radially arranged needles that are hard to the touch. "You should see where they grow in Spain — on the bare rocks high up in the mountains," she

says. Another favorite is *Abies koreana,* which "even when very young produces lovely cones that stand erect on the branches."

Hollies of all kinds are winter winners and another of Polly's enthusiasms. She took up the cause of the native winterberry (*Ilex verticillata*) and over the years singled out seven cultivars for introduction. "They differ in such ways as early or late fruiting; in the colors of their berries — crimson, red, or orange; in the size of their fruits; and in their plant height. The Vineyard strain has proved to be tough, exceptionally drought tolerant, and highly stoloniferous," she explains.

Besides her selections of deciduous holly, there are the evergreen hollies. One of her favorites is longstalk holly, *Ilex pedunculosa,* "which makes a fine ornamental shrub or small tree during any season." The leaves are not barbed but oval, rather like the leaves of mountain laurel, and the red fruits dangle invitingly on their long pedicels.

English Christmas card holly, *Ilex aquifolium,* is at the edge of its northern range on Martha's Vineyard. Nevertheless, twenty-foot trees are growing at Barnard's Inn Farm. Mirrored in their gleaming satin foliage, the red fruits are doubly effective. The American holly, *Ilex opaca,* is not quite as refined, and the leaves are less glossy, but in the hands of Elizabeth McFadden, Polly's gifted pruner and right hand, it gets "a lovely architectural look." Moreover, Polly has selected and introduced several cultivars that she regards as superior forms.

Until my visit to Martha's Vineyard, it was not clear to me that Polly had gained her reputation in horticulture as a grower and selector, not as a hybridizer. Hybridizers make crosses between plants of the same species, and sometimes between similar but different species. She expresses admiration for these dedicated plant breeders: "They are hardworking professionals for the most part, or dedicated amateurs. And they work with enormous numbers of crosses, which I don't. I borrow time as an ally to make up for my less creative approach."

It hardly seems less creative to me to devote forty-odd years to exploiting nature's potential in pursuit of new and better garden plants. Who knows what wonders have gone unseen because a rabbit devoured an infant plant that might have produced an unusual flower or a new color break? As a grower, Polly has aided and abetted nature by warding off rabbits, removing weeds, and providing ideal growing conditions for seedlings from both wild and cultivated plants.

With the utmost vigilance, she watches over immature trees and shrubs until they begin to show their qualities. Then, as a selector, she evaluates their performance in the garden — their form and habit, fruit and flowers — and ruthlessly discards all but the best. In this way she has chosen dozens of new, improved cultivars of holly, dogwood, magnolia, and stewartia.

Alas, not many of Polly's named selections have yet reached the public. Although she distributes them without charge to interested nurseries, it takes time to propagate enough clones to offer for sale. Moreover, many nurseries are reluctant to carry plants that are unfamiliar to the gardening public.

It is not surprising, therefore, that she is best known for her azaleas, which are familiar plants, popular with landscapers and gardeners alike. Often listed as North Tisbury azaleas — North Tisbury being a local name for Polly's area of Martha's Vineyard — these azaleas are hybrids of *Rhododendron nakaharae,* a dwarf, mound-forming, evergreen species endemic to Taiwan. The Nakaharae hybrids and their origins are woven into the fabric of Polly's personal and horticultural history.

The fourth of six children, Polly grew up on several acres in Ardmore, Pennsylvania, on the Main Line. To her, it seemed like the country. There were wildflowers, and the land was wooded. Her father loved trees, and when her family moved to the property there were many old American chestnuts, which subsequently died. It was her father's job to cut them up and stack them for firewood. She recalled his pleasure in the task: "He commuted by train to Philadelphia, but as soon as he got home from work, he changed into old clothes and went out to split logs. We used to have wonderful hissing, spitting fires made with the chestnut logs. Often someone had to snatch away the hearth rug to save it from the sparks."

Polly speaks affectionately of her parents, particularly her father, whom she characterizes as "a 'people person' with great insight and integrity." I learned that her father liked music, which may have influenced Polly's choice of a major at Vassar College. What her father did not like was her determination to go to Japan after graduation in 1928 to teach at Vassar's sister college, Tokyo Joshi Daigaku. But he assented, however reluctantly. During the year she spent there, Polly studied flower arranging — not because she was particularly interested in the subject, but because it gave her a bond with the students she was expected to teach. Little did she know at that time what an impact Japan would have on her future.

After she returned home, she married Julian Hill and moved with him to Wilmington, Delaware. As a young married woman and the mother of small children, she had two choices of extracurricular activity — antiques at nearby Winterthur or gardens at Longwood. Her decision was swift, and her reason simple: "Longwood was alive and new, so I went that way." After World War II, Longwood Gardens began offering courses in horticulture, and Polly availed herself of this opportunity. As she became increasingly serious about plants, she spent another two years taking botany, taxonomy, and plant pathology at the University of Delaware.

Then, in 1956, she made a second trip to Japan. By this time her interest in horticulture had crystalized, and she arrived with a letter of introduction from Longwood's director, Dr. Russell Seibert, to Dr. Tsuneshige Rokujo. As she had her fifteen-year-old son and a friend in tow, her time was limited, but she met Dr. Rokujo for half a day. He was a surgeon by profession but a hybridizer of rhododendrons by avocation, and they found much in common. In a few hours they established an enduring rapport and a productive horticultural alliance.

After Polly's return to the United States, they kept in touch. As she tells it, "We began corresponding, and he asked me what I wanted that he could send me. I remembered the low-growing azaleas tucked into the base of a rock in a temple yard. I told him we had no low-growing azaleas, only big bushes, so he crossed his *nakaharae* with various cultivars in his collection to please me. He came up with seeds of three or four of my present selections, all carefully documented for both parents, plus one group of open-pollinated seed from which I selected 'Wintergreen', 'Marilee', and 'Nakami'." Polly describes this group as low, tightly twigged, and mounding in form. 'Wintergreen' is so called for its good green winter color. Other Nakaharae hybrids turn maroon in leaf and bud.

'Pink Pancake', a name familiar even to the average gardener, belonged to the first group. Resulting from a cross between a cultivated variety in Dr. Rokojo's garden and the species *nakaharae*, it is one of the flattest of flat ground-covering azaleas, with large, slightly frilled blossoms of shrimp pink. The good doctor sent Polly the seeds; she grew them, "chose the best, and chucked the others." 'Late Love', also pink, and 'Michael Hill', a bright salmon pink, were among those she saved.

If you don't know these hardy, ground-hugging, evergreen azaleas, you have a treat in store. Dense with tiny lacquered dark green leaves, they look like miniature landscapes of rolling hills. Under two feet high but spreading to as much as thirteen feet by eight feet, they have proportionally large flowers. Many of the cultivars have red flowers, like the species *nakaharae*.

At Barnard's Inn Farm, treasured plants are protected by a tall post and woven-wire fence enclosing an area three hundred feet long and thirty-five feet wide. Polly's husband, Julian, christened it the Playpen, and it was here that we made the longest stop on my all-too-fleeting visit. I was shown the original plant of *Rhododendron nakaharae*, the species from which the North Tisbury hybrids are derived. The story goes that in 1969, a friend from the Vineyard took her children to Taiwan to be near her husband, who was based in Vietnam. Little anticipating success, Polly asked her to keep an eye peeled for the wild *R. nakaharae*. While picnicking on Mount Seven Star, one of the children literally stumbled upon the sought-after plant.

"My friend got somebody to collect the seed, and she passed it on to me," Polly explained. "From that seed, two germinated, and one lived. That is *the* plant." She indicated a low mass of fine foliage. A similar plant, 'Joseph Hill', named for her son, is purportedly the hybrid most like the species from Mount Seven Star. It is also one of the most widely available of her azaleas.

A year after Polly's second Japanese trip, her mother died, leaving Barnard's Inn Farm to the Hills. They managed the farm for her father, who urged them to make use of the surrounding fields in any way they saw fit. At that time Julian planted a large family vegetable garden and Polly prepared her first nursery bed for seedlings. Recalling this modest start, she said, "Seed is the cheapest way to grow things, and that way you learn and get to know the plants." It is this intimate knowledge of plants from fruit to flower — a journey sometimes taking thirty years — that elevates Polly to the status of plantswoman.

She has received innumerable awards, among them the Arthur Hoyt Scott Garden and Horticultural Award from Swarthmore College and medals from the Pennsylvania Horticultural Society, the Massachusetts Horticultural Society, and the American Rhododendron Society. A research scientist supporting her Rhododendron Society citation described her as "a disciplined researcher." Wise, down-to-earth, and not easily impressed, Polly refers to herself as "a simple gardener."

Joanna Reed

"There is so much to see in the winter," says Joanna Reed. "In the summer the woods are just a mass of green, but in the wintertime you can pick out the individual trees — sassafras with its fat buds, young beeches that hang on to their silver-gilt leaves, and the tulip poplars with all those seed heads, like candles on a birthday cake. In the winter you get excited about little things — the mere shape of the trees. Some are all twiggy, and some are big and stark and rugged. The katsura (*Cercidiphyllum japonicum*) has a nice elegance to its silhouette, while the Kentucky coffee tree (*Gymnocladus dioicus*) is strong-looking, with heavy branches — even the young branches are thick and heavy."

An adventurous and original gardener, Joanna grows many unusual trees at Longview Farm in Malvern, Pennsylvania. A few years ago, she lost the arborescent star of her winter garden to a tornado. *Idesia polycarpa,* a native of the Far East, grows to fifty feet with wide-spreading tiered branches. In early summer, tiny yellow flowers are borne on both male and female trees. Those of the female ripen into scarlet fruits. Joanna described their effect in the essay she contributed to Ellen Samuels and Rosemary Verey's book *The American Woman's Garden:* "This tree is gloriously festooned through the fall and winter with long panicles of bright red fruits, a veritable garden Cinderella after its nondescript spring and summer green."

For a time, she thought that the idesia would recover from the tornado damage. She told me, "It had only lost a couple of limbs, but the roots must have been very twisted by the storm. Within two years it was dead. However, I already had a seedling coming along. It hasn't been pollinated yet, but I think it's a female, and I've found about five other seedlings, so I'm sure one of them will pollinate it."

A short time before my visit, another twister had cut a devastating path through the property. I was appalled by the mess. Trees were down everywhere. Some had been topped; others had lost huge limbs, and the woodland paths were strewn with debris. "I have my winter work cut out for me," Joanna remarked matter-of-factly. "The township has lifted its ban on fires to facilitate cleanup. I'll burn the brush, either when there's snow on the ground or else in a light rain. I just put on a sou'wester and go out there like a troll. When I have a burn pile, I'll stay out there until after dark."

For fifty years Joanna has been cleaning up the Pennsylvania countryside. During the early days she also brought up five children and farmed about a hundred acres. Together with her husband, she raised pigs and chickens, sold eggs, and grew everything the family ate. All the while, in her spare time, she planted trees, shrubs, bulbs, perennials, and wildflowers.

When her husband died a dozen years ago, she assumed the entire responsibility for keeping up Longview Farm. Although the pigs and chickens have long since gone, the amount of work is still enormous. Joanna's son, who lives next door, offered to mow the five-acre field and do the lawns, but she said, "You've got your own life. Just be around when I need you for the big things." By "big things," she meant tree removal and major cleanup after storms. She does the mowing with a Gravely tractor. "I love it," she says. "I'm like an old cow — I ruminate when I mow."

There is always something to be done, and during the winter it is not unusual for Joanna to spend the whole day in the woods. She enjoys these close encounters with her landscape. "You get to know your land that way," she says. "When I first started working here, I thought, 'This is a dumb little woods.' The trees were all fairly young then, and to me the ground looked flat. But after several winters I realized that the land rolls. There are high places and low places and much more contour than I first thought. It was only by working in the woods and getting to know the terrain that I made this discovery. When it's not all draped in greenery, you see the bones of it."

Appreciative of winter's special delights, Joanna observes with satisfaction that a little clump of partridgeberry (*Mitchella repens*), which her brother gave her in a terrarium, has spread into large patches throughout the woods. Every year she finds a new spot where its trailing stems, paired round leaves, and bright berries have made a carpet of dark green flecked with red. She enjoys all the ground covers at this time of year, particularly the epimediums, which turn bronze and retain their foliage until March, and the bergenias, with handsome, paddle-shaped leaves that assume a rosy tint in the winter.

Helleborus foetidus is another favorite, because it forms promising buds just as most other herbaceous perennials are going dormant. The clusters of pale green flowers edged in red open in December and last for weeks. "When it gets really cold, the stems lie down on the ground, but as soon as the temperature gets above twenty degrees, they stand up again," Joanna notes. "Even when the flowers are over, the sepals and seedpods are almost as interesting, and they look good right up until April or May."

Along the woodland paths, beneath the swaths of epimedium, bergenia, and hellebore, thousands of snowdrops and winter aconites await a warm spell in February to push through the ground. Rhododendrons (*Rhododendron maximum*) and leucothoes (*Leucothoe catesbaei*) rise above the bulbs and perennials. As Joanna points out, "Because I live in such a windy spot, I can't have any broadleaf evergreens near the house. So I have them in the woods, where they are sheltered among the trees. In the summer you are not aware of them, but in the winter they suddenly stand out, delineating the paths and leading you into the rest of the woods." She also planted witch hazels (*Hamamelis mollis*) along the paths, with the idea that they would weave a yellow thread among the broadleaf evergreens, but the deer were uncooperative, and these shrubs have not yet bloomed. However, *Hamamelis vernalis* grows nearer the house and perfumes the February air with its sharp, sweet scent.

In addition to the woodland plantings, there is the garden proper. In the American sense, it is not one garden but many. Joanna's first efforts at ornamental gardening resulted in a small formal garden adjacent to the huge vegetable plot that once fed the family. (Today it is an equally huge flower garden). It is square, bounded on one side by a former garage that has been remodeled as a house for her youngest son and his family. On the strength of sound advice — "A friend who was a great gardener said, 'If you start doing any symmetrical thing, tie it in with something that is already in existence'" — the fledgling garden-maker united building and garden with low retaining walls on three sides. She laid every stone herself, and when she was finished, she added a garden bench as a focal point.

One garden soon led to another, and another: the secret barnyard garden, with a cistern that became a lily pool; a parterre garden below the house, which can be looked down on from the porch; and a little walled entryway garden. The walls are beautiful in themselves. Built of local stone in shades of cream, gray, and cinnamon brown, they enclose a courtyard paved in matching pebbles. These were purchased by one of the local garden clubs for a display at the Philadelphia Flower Show. Afterward, the Reeds bought the pebbles from the club.

Mixed plantings of perennials, shrubs, and trees border a long sweep of lawn that unfolds from the house westward toward the woodland garden. "When we bought the property in 1940, the land was open except for that little maple woods," Joanna explains. Now a thickly planted strip of trees to the north shuts out the sight and muffles the sound of the Pennsylvania Turnpike. Joanna began planting trees there in 1950, when the Reeds' property was bisected by the turnpike. She is philosophical about it: "It's not a bad neighbor, because the cars keep moving. It's better than a subdivision." She still owns ten acres on the other side of the road, once part of the long view from which the farm took its name.

"Everything you see between the house and the turnpike, we planted," she says. "The first screen we put in died after about fourteen years, because the ground got wetter and wetter. But a few loblolly pines survived. They were given to me by a brother who had a farm in Delaware. He was reforesting, so he gave me a little bundle of ten of them."

Joanna has watched the development of this new woodland with great interest. In addition to the species that she and her husband first planted, there are now self-sown seedlings from the nearby woodland. Maple saplings were shortly followed by tulip poplars and ash. Already the ash is on the wane, while the number of shagbark hickories seems to be increasing. "The woods are going through their natural progression," she observes. "But I didn't think I'd see it so soon. It's kind of a bonus."

Joanna's love of woody plants dates back to a chance meeting with Dr. Albert C. Barnes, of the Barnes Arboretum. Dr. Barnes and his wife, Laura, were a brilliant, eccentric, civic-minded couple possessed of diverse gifts, great altruism, and great wealth. A chemist and physician by training, Dr. Barnes never actually practiced medicine. He and a colleague developed a preparation for relieving nasal congestion called Argerol nose drops. When Joanna and I were growing up, children's head colds were routinely treated with this dark brown stuff, which ran down the back of one's throat, tasted foul, and made hankies disgusting.

Barnes owned the factory that manufactured Argerol, and it proved lucrative enough to finance a fine collection of art and an educational program for his factory workers that made him a pioneer in continuing education. Joanna's admiration for this effort is unbounded: "It was a wonderful, generous thing that they did. It began with classes for the workers in Dr. Barnes's factory. They would decide among themselves — everyone from the sweeper to his secretary — what they wanted to learn, then he would get in professors to teach whatever they chose. That was part of their paid workday. And it didn't cost a cent."

In 1922, Dr. Barnes bought the estate of Joseph Lapsley Wilson as a setting for his art treasures. According to Joanna, Mr. Wilson had been loath to sell because of the trees he had spent a lifetime collecting, including rare specimens from all over the world. But the Barneses assured him that the trees would be cared for, and he agreed to the sale. From that moment on, Mrs. Barnes, who had always liked gardening, became fascinated with trees. She enrolled in classes in botany, horticulture, and landscape architecture at the University of Pennsylvania. To give others a similar opportunity, she established a school. The Barnes Foundation, in Merion, Pennsylvania, continues to provide instruction in those subjects dear to her heart.

"I will forever be grateful to Mrs. Barnes," says Joanna. "She provided all these marvelous professors. We had Jack Fogg, who was a world-class botanist. We had Henry Skinner, who ended up with the Veitch Medal of Honor. She provided all that by having her school and sharing it and asking nothing whatsoever in return." In later years, Joanna and Mrs. Barnes became friends. "We laughingly used to call this place her annex, because almost all of our woodies came from her. It was a wonderful thing for me to fall into. And I fell into it because Dr. Barnes had car trouble."

Joanna and her husband, George, were newlyweds when Dr. and Mrs. Barnes began restoring a country house down the road from Longview Farm. En route to the property, the Barneses' car broke down, and the doctor appeared at the Reeds' door to ask to use the phone. While waiting for the towtruck, he inquired whether they planned to have a garden.

Joanna recalls saying that she would like one but didn't know how to get started. At that point, he told her about the Barnes Arboretum.

Much later, when Mrs. Barnes was in failing health, Joanna and George stopped by for a brief visit. They had just been awarded a certificate from the Pennsylvania Horticulture Society for their vegetable garden and knew that Mrs. Barnes would be pleased. As they were preparing to leave, she said, "I have gotten such satisfaction from the school. Now it's up to you people to carry on, to keep this going and return what you have gotten out of it." By opening her own garden for visitors, Joanna feels that she is fulfilling her charge from Mrs. Barnes: "I feel very closely allied to her in doing this. It's wonderful to feel that you are a link in a chain."

Another link in the gardening chain goes back further than Mrs. Barnes, to a grandmother who made hollyhock dolls for her grandchildren and had a lovely garden in West Virginia. "My mother's mother really loved gardens," Joanna remembers. "She had what she used to call spider-web parties for her grandchildren — there were nine of us. Everybody would get a present, which would be hidden in the garden, tied to a string. You had to untangle all these strings, which were woven together, but you were not allowed to walk in the garden. When I got older, I used to visit her and sit in the pergola and read. I know all that influenced me."

When Joanna was small, the family lived near her grandmother. But after her mother's tragically early death, her father moved them to Philadelphia, so the children could attend better schools. Despite his own problems and the Depression, which was then in full swing, he did well by his family. Joanna recalls, "Because I liked gardens, he used to take me to Garden Week in Virginia. And though he didn't garden himself, he introduced me to beautiful things — to design and the rest of it, which I absorbed unconsciously. My father provided a very rich life for us all."

He was able to do this with the help of an admirable German woman, who had come to the family two years before Joanna was born and took care of all three children until they were grown. Once they were launched, she stayed on to keep house for Joanna's father, remaining with him until her death. "She was a surrogate mother and a wonderful lady," says Joanna, "and in later years we had a grand time with each other." But with children, she was a stern taskmaster who "never made anything too pleasurable or easy." Joanna remembers learning to sew. Every stitch had to be perfect, "and because she was German, everything had to be utilitarian. So I learned to darn my brother's socks — and I hated it!" It makes her laugh to think back on these early struggles, but the rigorous training paid unexpected dividends later when she wanted to learn crewelwork.

She became interested after seeing an exhibit of crewel embroidery based on Jacobean designs. The technique interested her, and she decided to take a class. The teacher set her students to work on sampler pillows, which Joanna completed with ease. "After a while, I said I'd like to make curtains, but I was assured that I was not ready. I thought to myself, 'If I make one more pillow, I'll give up the whole thing!' My oldest daughter, who had suggested my doing crewelwork in the first place, knew where I could get the material, and I began doing it like bootleg work at home. When I was two thirds finished, I took the curtains in to the teacher, and she was flabbergasted."

Word of Joanna's embroidered curtains reached my ears weeks before my visit to Longview Farm. A young friend working at nearby Longwood Gardens had raved about the exquisite design of twining flowers, leaves, acorns, berries, and cones. "It was going to be Jacobean designs, because that's what they taught at the school where I studied," Joanna explains. "Then George suggested that I do natural things. In the end, I would go out and pick something and draw from that piece. I never did a color sketch, because I saw that in my head. But I drew the whole design first on brown paper. Then I would do a section at a time, tracing just the rudiments onto the curtains and stitching from the subject so that I could add by eye." And what an eye! In the winter, Joanna gardens indoors with fine worsted yarn.

An artist in and out of the garden, she attributes her pleasure and success as a needlewoman and as a gardener to educational experiences. "I was so lucky — first to go to the Philadelphia Museum School of Industrial Art for two years, then the Barnes Foundation, with wonderful professors. We learned about the history of gardens, about the plant explorers, where the plants came from. It was a full story. And when I learned about sewing, I learned how to do it right. It all goes together, and for practicality, I had this wonderful neighbor who taught me how to work hard."

Isaiah Cuff was a local farmer who took the young Reeds in hand when they arrived at Longview Farm. He observed that they were an industrious pair eager to do right by their land. Figuring that a couple who owned a hay rake, a mower, and a tractor might as well profit from their efforts, he persuaded them to farm instead of just keeping the fields open. As Joanna remembers, "George said he didn't know anything about farming. But Cuffy said, 'I'll tell you what to do. It's better for your land.'"

One of Joanna's chores during the farming years was to help Cuffy clear the two thousand feet of hedgerows surrounding the property. She would clip and he would saw. On the first day, she had looked, aghast, down a seemingly endless stretch of brush. "I said, 'We're never going to get this finished!' But he said, 'Now, wait a minute. You have to learn a very important thing. You never look at what you have to do — look only at your finished work. Back into the rest.' And I've been backing into life ever since. I tell other people that this is the best way not to get discouraged. But I forget it sometimes. Without Cuffy, it could have been overwhelming."

Planned for Winter

Plants alone do not a winter garden make. Like the beauty of actress Katharine Hepburn, beauty in the winter season depends on bone structure. While a summer garden may have the beguiling loveliness of an ingenue, all pink complexion and yielding softness, a garden built on the skillful orchestration of structural elements holds up in any season. And in the winter, such a garden comes into its own.

Line suddenly becomes important, because everything shows — the outline of beds and the edges and direction of paths. The intersections of vertical and horizontal planes become clearly visible: the meeting of walls with the ground, with the horizon, and with each other. The slant of a roof makes a geometric pattern against the sky, and skeletal trees draw linear shadows on the ground.

Form is the language of the leafless season. Evergreens dusted with snow stand out in three dimensions, as cones, spheres, cubes, rectangles. Details and textures come into focus: frost rims a leaf, or snow caps a seedpod. Color is important too, but even the tiniest flash of bright color — a berried twig or a cardinal's feathers — becomes electrifying among the restrained hues of winter.

In the summer garden, flowers and foliage can cover a multitude of sins. Who cares if the perennial bed is the shape of a kidney bean and has no relationship to the rest of the back yard? It overflows with blossoms in iridian tints and delights the senses. In the winter, however, the same bed shows up as a meaningless brown scar in the lawn. Deciduous trees and shrubs can disguise an ugly garage or hide the compost pile with handsome foliage during the growing season, but as soon as the leaves fall, these necessities are revealed as the eyesores they are.

For a garden to be effective in winter, it has to have good bones. And gardeners with a strong sense of design are hands-down winners. *A Dictionary of Landscape Architecture* defines "design" as "the creative laying-out and planning of the outdoor space for the greatest possible amount of harmony, utility, and beauty."

In a garden, harmony becomes visible when the parts are fitted together to form a connected whole, and what shows in the absence of leaves and flowers is relationships. You see the buildings — house, garage, and outbuildings — in relation to the site; the deck or terrace, steps and paths, in relation to the buildings; and the sum of these manmade structures in relation to the surrounding terrain.

If there is order and purpose in the relationships, the onlooker experiences a sense of satisfaction, like a sigh of relief. You know where to go and what to look at. Paths have a destination, and terraces have a view. Boundaries separate the wild landscape from the garden and tell you where you are.

Garden designer Lynden Miller has a practical liking for hedges and fences as boundaries and a whimsical fondness for the story of Peter and the wolf. "I have always loved the idea that you have to stay inside the gate," she says, "because it is civilized within and wild without. That's how I tried to make my garden. All the adventures and wildness are outside the formal hedge." In this chapter, she shares her thoughts on maintaining seasonal beauty and her approach to garden-making.

Lynden B. Miller

It is no wonder that Karen Bussolini took so many pictures in Lynden Miller's winter garden: there are so many pictures to take. What Lynden does in her garden, she does so well that you don't know she is doing it. But from the moment you arrive at the gate, you unwittingly put yourself in her hands. An artist first and a garden designer second, she presents you with a series of pictures. Gently but firmly, she directs your gaze to scenes she has either created or selected. She draws your footsteps along predestined paths and determines the order in which you will experience the garden.

Leaving your car in the driveway, you are immediately confronted with a picture. The view, framed by lattice panels and the beautiful curved arch of the gate, is like a cameo — a small, clearly defined scene centering on a matched pair of conical evergreens. In the winter, snow emphasizes their solid forms. Pale grasses in the perennial border trace a vertical design against the backdrop of dark hedge and slate-blue hills.

In the immediate foreground, a *Pieris japonica* stops the eye with its gracefully drooping clusters of red flower buds, ready and waiting for spring. Nothing else can be seen through the opening of the gate — just the pieris and that one little corner of the garden. The rest is blocked by a huge mugo pine. Your appetite whetted by this introduction, you immediately want to see more. But in order to discover the garden, you have to step inside.

When you skirt the bulk of the mugo pine, you suddenly see the whole satisfying curve of the perfectly groomed yew hedge. This magnificent hedge describes an arc on the northwest side of the house, embracing perennial borders and a serene sweep of lawn. Even in winter the borders are rich with color. But your appreciative gaze is not yet allowed to wander among the shrubs, grasses, and perennials. It is immediately drawn to an old crab-apple tree whose canopy has been pruned into a twiggy umbrella. With every twig rimmed in snow, it is breathtaking.

The background hedge is pierced by three openings, each with a gate and, on either side, matching upright evergreens. An aerial view would reveal the underlying geometry of the garden. Grassy paths radiate from the hub of the semicircular hedge and fan out into the fields beyond. Innocent of this arrangement, the visitor is lured to each of the three openings in turn.

The first leads down an allée of crab-apple trees to a garden bench. But your eye cannot avoid a detour to the left to delight in a small board-and-lattice structure that houses garden tools. The building has solid, waist-high white wooden walls with lattice above. Recessed arches embellish the back and side walls and repeat the curves that are a theme in many of the gates and other garden structures. "I repeat that shape all around," says Lynden. "Even in the benches." On one side of the toolhouse is a little octagonal garden with a stone plinth in the center, and on the other the nursery garden, enclosed with a white board fence. Although it is supposed to be a place to experiment with plants, the nursery is also pleasing to the eye in all seasons. Not the least of its winter attractions is a tall weathered wooden post topped by an armillary sphere.

Returning from that visual excursion, you pass along the perennial border to reach the next opening in the hedge. Now you have an opportunity to dawdle and admire the richness of Lynden's winter planting. The tall ornamental grasses are blond and beautiful. Ghostly gray stems of perovskia stand out against the solid reddish brown shapes of a barberry hung with scarlet fruit. If you hadn't yet noticed the flat brown flowerheads of *Sedum* 'Autumn Joy', you do now, and, on closer inspection, the low, spiky mounds of silver-blue *Helictotrichon sempervirens,* which retains its color all winter.

The principal opening in the hedge is identified by a handsome arch with a gate, which Lynden copied from an old photograph of a garden on Long Island. Through this frame, you look down the major axis of the garden to a pergola. Lynden refers to this structure as the Temple. "We needed something out in the field to go to," she says, "even if you didn't go to it." The columns for the Temple were salvaged by her husband, Leigh, during the renovations on their nineteenth-century house. The white pergola stands out against a background of pines, which blend into the natural woodland. A blue mountain peak rises in the far distance. "I put the gate opening here," says Lynden, "because I wanted the top of the mountain to the right, not straight on."

The final breach in the hedge leads to the swimming pool. "I went out and found another gate, similar to this one but a little different," Lynden explains. Even the pool enclosure has a garden feeling, thanks to a white picket fence and artful plantings. From the gate, the focus for viewers is the poolhouse, with its lattice walls, open arch, and a pair of wooden chairs — inviting in the summer, haunting in the winter.

If there is such a thing as a perfect garden, this is it. The spaces and structures have a pleasing relationship to the house and to each other. There are many separate elements, but they are related to the whole. The style is neither formal nor informal. It is pictorial, as befits the garden of an artist. In the winter landscape, the hedge and the alignment of the paths, the fences, the outbuildings, and other structural features are very important. But to a painter turned garden designer, so are the subtle colors of the season.

I have now seen Lynden's garden in all weathers and at different times of the year. It is always beautiful. When I told her about this book, she generously agreed to share her thoughts on the subject of gardens in winter. We met on a Sunday morning in June, and she took me around, pointing out favorite plants for winter color. Recalling that occasion during a recent February visit, I felt as if I had looked up the answers to a quiz in the back of the book. Everything that she had said that summer morning took on new meaning.

"This is *Ilex glabra*," she began. "You don't notice it now among all the flowers and other greenery, but it is there for winter. I have a lot of evergreens in the main border, which you don't pay much attention to in the summer. But they're wonderful in the winter. The juniper is there because it is blue, and the rose because it has scarlet hips. And I use red-twig dogwood [*Cornus alba* 'Elegantissima'] — I couldn't live without that in a garden."

The architectural elements of the plants, the Temple, and snow make a study in black and white in Lynden Miller's garden.

Nature's monochromatic study includes one manmade element, the white wooden bench.

The first picture seen from the entrance to Lynden's garden centers on matched plantings of *Thuja occidentalis* 'Degroot's Emerald Spire', with globes of *Ilex glabra,* sheaves of *Miscanthus sinensis* 'Gracillimus', and clumps of *Sedum* 'Autumn Joy' in the winter border.

Lynden Miller works in a south-facing alcove off the kitchen.

Opposite: Perovskia atriplicifolia,
Miscanthus sinensis 'Variegatus', and
the twiggy, berry-flecked barberry
(*Berberis thunbergii* 'Rose Glow')
make a handsome winter trio.

The view of Ragna Goddard's topiary garden
from the attic window includes the central feature
of this garden-within-a-garden: the fountain.

The intricate pattern of Ragna's knot garden
is highlighted by a dusting of snow.

A chickadee drinks from the author's heated birdbath.

The fruit of *Viburnum trilobum* overhangs a split rail fence in Christine Utterback's bird garden.

Opposite: In this corner of Jack and June Dunbar's garden, seen from the upper deck, rhododendrons and hollies form an evergreen background and ground cover for the weeping beech (*Fagus sylvatica* 'Pendula').

Winterberry (*Ilex verticillata*) makes a finely textured, colorful display against ornamental grasses and spirea. *Below:* Christine's desk also functions as her favorite birdwatching post.

She was excited about a recent introduction that had been in her nursery garden for three years, *Cornus sericea* 'Silver and Gold'. The leaves are edged in white, and the stems are a startling golden yellow. She plans to move it into the main border next year. Thinking out loud, she said, "Maybe I could put the yellow and red together."

Moving on, she gestured toward *Berberis thunbergii* 'Rose Glow'. "The barberries are for every season, but they are especially good in winter because I clip them gently into round shapes. When you look at a garden, it's all going like this." She indicated an upright fountain shape with her hands. "Most plants read as vertical stems. I think you also need to take some plants and make them into rounds."

Some of Lynden's most effective winter plants also make a substantial contribution to the summer garden. The new leaves of the barberry 'Rose Glow' are pink spattered with the wine color of the mature foliage. Red-stemmed *Rosa* 'Thérèse Bugnet' is a disease-resistant shrub rose with attractive foliage and pink blossoms, and both the yellow- and the red-twig dogwoods boast variegated leaves that double for flowers.

The marvelous yew hedge, meticulously sheared by Leigh, is the glory of this garden in any season, but in winter it comes into its own as a structure. It is also important as a background for other plants. "I look at the outline of plants against it," says Lynden. "I like negative and positive spaces, and what I see in my mind is the green shape of the hedge around the plants. If there are not enough interesting ups and downs, rounds and verticals, then it isn't right, and I go out and take something down or trim something."

She begins preparing the garden for winter in October, postponing the removal of hosta leaves until their rich golden ocher fades. Other perennials she cuts to the ground in November. Still others are allowed to stand all winter: the wheat-colored grasses, the rigid brown skeletons of phlox and sedum, and the pale stems of the perovskia. The focal point of the main border is the old crab apple, its carefully pruned crown echoing the curves of the archways.

Lynden loves this tree and was thrilled when Leigh gave her an outdoor lighting system one Christmas. At night the tree and the three gates are illuminated. "While I take pleasure in the lighting all year round, it is really wonderful in the winter," she says. "I light the garden at five o'clock and have the fun of looking at my structures all evening."

She delights in the winter aspect of all the architectural elements, particularly a pair of graceful wooden posts that stand on either side of one of the gates. "They look heavenly in the snow," she says. "Once it was so deep that it came up to the base of the finials. They looked exactly like sherbet glasses — the kind they used to have at Shrafft's for those huge ice cream sundaes."

As we looked through the main archway toward the Temple, she drew my attention to the closely mowed grass path cutting through the untamed field. "In the winter, I keep the path mowed right up until the last possible minute, so that you see the contrast of the smooth against the rough of the field." Months later, I admired the effect. Light snow frosted the hummocks of field grass but lay more thickly on the shorn path, which now stretched in a white band from the gate to the Temple. I recalled something Lynden had said about how a garden needs paths, hedges, and fences: "As a painter, you use these strong lines to hold together a lot of scattered shapes."

The tradition of art and gardening has been a recurring theme in Lynden's life and in her family. "My grandmother painted beautiful botanical stuff," she says, "and my uncle was an architect. He really should have been a landscape architect, because he was always carving out gardens, and he used to let me help him." These early influences eventually blossomed into a career that fuses art, architecture, and horticulture. Art came first.

Lynden studied the history of art as an undergraduate, but an interest in politics and a strong social conscience drew her toward Washington, D.C., after she graduated from Smith College, in Northampton, Massachusetts. Soon, however, she met Leigh and returned to her first love, painting. She enrolled in the master's degree program at the University of Maryland and began turning out large, colorful canvases and collages.

"I was very much influenced both by abstract expressionism and by the color of Persian miniatures and Matisse paintings," she says. "I studied a lot about color. My paintings and collages are very colorful, although I did a lot of etching too. I *loved* etching — always natural forms. There's always a landscape if you look."

Without knowing it, Lynden was building the scaffolding for her career as a garden designer, and today, when young people ask her how to prepare for the profession, she says, "Study art history and take drawing. You should go and look in museums and see how artists put paintings together, because a garden is just the same — it's about line and form, texture and proportion of color."

Long before Lynden recognized the connections between art and horticulture, she turned her hand to planting gardens. In the sixties, she and Leigh had a house in Washington — "a sweet house, white brick with an apple tree. I tried to make gardens all over the place, but the lawnmower man mowed everything down. I was totally incompetent anyway. I'd never taken a course, and I didn't know the name of anything. I just knew that I terribly wanted a garden."

A short time later the Millers left the white brick house and moved to New York City. A native New Yorker, Lynden nonetheless yearned for a country house where she could have a garden. In 1971, when the younger of their two sons was six months old, they found a place in Columbia County, New York. Lynden immediately set about making a border. She told a more sophisticated gardening friend that she wanted lots of color. The friend smiled indulgently, said she would grow out of that notion, and plied her with books by Gertrude Jekyll and Vita Sackville-West.

Another friend suggested that she take a course with the illustrious T. H. Everett at the New York Botanical Garden. Mr. Everett and the librarian, Elizabeth Hall, were impressed by Lynden's promise and became her mentors. She also received encouragement at home. In 1972, Leigh arranged a tour of English gardens that opened up a new world. Four years later, the

Millers found themselves living in London. "We went there," Leigh explains, "because I was working for American Express Bank at the time, and I was sent to be managing director of their London merchant bank."

They bought a house in Bedford Gardens, in Kensington. It was a late Georgian row house with a small garden in the front and a small garden in the back, and Lynden wanted to do something with it. "I tried fooling with it by myself and didn't get anywhere. So I telephoned Miss Hall and Mr. Everett. Miss Hall — you know how friendly and adorable she was — told me to call up Lanning Roper. I said I couldn't just call up Lanning Roper. But she said, 'Oh yes, you could. You tell him Mr. Everett and I said that you should speak to him.'"

American though he was, Lanning Roper was one of the most admired garden designers in Britain from the mid-fifties until his death in 1983. He was also an accessible sort of person, but Lynden was too awed by his reputation to call him. Instead she wrote him a respectful note saying that she had had a garden at home but was now living in England. She added that she would be grateful if he could recommend someone who might advise her about plant material for her London garden.

Even now, Lynden marvels at the outcome of her daring. "I sent the note off on a Tuesday and by return post received a reply saying, 'I'll be right over. When's tea?' The children were small then, so I got somebody to watch them while I made paper-thin oatmeal cookies." Roper ate the cookies and made suggestions, but before offering his advice, he asked about the style of Lynden's paintings. "I took him upstairs to look at my collages," she recalls. "He looked at all of them and said, 'I understand — careless rapture, that's what you want.' Then he and I laughed, because of course 'careless rapture' is very hard to achieve."

Although Lynden continued to paint and etch during the London years, the transition from painter to garden designer was well under way by the time she returned to America. Coming home had its own rewards. Just before leaving for England, the Millers bought a country house in Connecticut. Upon their return, they threw themselves into developing their property and beating back the jungle. When the trees, honeysuckle, and poison ivy had been cleared, Lynden began work on the garden that would become her design textbook.

The strands of her life as an artist are so interwoven with those of her work as a garden designer that she no longer thinks of them as separate. But that was not always the case. When her friend Betsy Rogers approached her in 1982 to restore the Conservatory Garden in New York City's Central Park, Lynden was overwhelmed.

"I said, 'You've got to be crazy! I wouldn't know how to do that.' And she said, 'Oh, sure you would. You've got horticultural knowledge and experience, and you're an artist. I want an artist's eye.' It hadn't crossed my mind at the time, but a garden *is* a collage. It never comes out quite as you planned it, and you change it on the spot. Collage and painting are just the same. And because of the years of training as a painter, I can visualize things in my head. I know what they are going to look like because I can make them stand up. I can visualize colors, textures, and contrasts easily. That's been a huge help to me."

As soon as she realized that she could approach the Conservatory Garden as a collage, Lynden was off and running. She made large collage pictures of what she had in mind for each individual garden. As she describes it, "What I do is to assemble collages from pictures cut out of catalogues, like the Wayside Gardens catalogue. I cut out the actual plant but change the scale. And it works very well." In fact, it works so well that she is constantly in demand as a garden designer here and abroad.

There is an alcove off the kitchen in the Millers' country house. It faces south and has many windows. A spiral staircase coils up to the second floor, and in the winter there are pots of semitender hellebores on every step. Geraniums and potted bulbs crowd the shelves of a metal stand. This is where the family has breakfast and lunch from October to April. Although it is hard to imagine Lynden sitting anywhere for long, this is also where she spends long winter afternoons reading and thinking about next season — and the next design project.

Ragna T. Goddard

During the summer and fall, the Sundial Herb Garden, in Higganum, Connecticut, is open to the public on Friday, Saturday, and Sunday and on other days by appointment. November and December, until Christmas Eve, are particularly busy in the shop and tearoom. After Christmas, Ragna and Tom Goddard tackle the mountains of paperwork that a small business entails. But at least the shop and tearoom are open only on weekends, so during the week the Goddards have the winter garden to themselves.

In their brochure, Ragna writes: "The Sundial Herb Garden had its beginning in 1970, when restoration of our eighteenth-century farmhouse aroused an interest not only in the architecture of the period but in the plantings as well." Little did either she or Tom dream at the time that a personal interest would spawn a full-time business. Both were graphic designers in the process of relocating from New York City to Connecticut. Tom had already joined American Education Publications in nearby Middletown, but Ragna was still going back and forth to New York once a week.

On a Friday night about six months after they acquired the house in Higganum, Tom returned from work to the sound of hammering and old plaster crashing to the floor. "My wife had decided to tear down a wall," he explains. "She said, 'This wall doesn't belong here.' She had been studying some books about period houses. And that really began the restoration." To German-born Ragna, "restoration" had a very specific meaning: "When the house and grounds become a unit, that's considered a true restoration."

As progress on the house moved forward, Ragna began eyeing the view beyond her windows. One of her grandfathers had been a botanist and her father had been a professor of ecology, so she already had an interest in plants. In addition, she had studied art and graphic design in Germany. Her teachers there had been influenced by the Bauhaus movement and favored a disciplined, no-frills approach that dictated her style of garden-making.

Given her background and an innate sensitivity to spacial relationships, she set about making an architectural garden based on interlocking geometric forms. Her research on period houses revealed that herb gardens were customary, so she planted herbs.

Before long, neighbors and friends began dropping in to see the herb garden. "Sometimes," Ragna recalls, "we would be in the house having breakfast, and total strangers would be roaming around the garden. We decided to structure some time and have the garden open on weekends so that we could get our other work done." The Sundial Herb Garden became a business in 1976, complete with shop and tearoom.

If Lynden Miller's garden-making is rooted in art and personal expression, Ragna's is allied to architecture and history. She prepared me for my first visit by saying that the design of her landscape was based on the Old World tradition of looking at gardens as part and parcel of the domestic architecture. She traced the connection between home and garden back in time to 3000 B.C., and in locale to the cradle of civilization.

Ragna's original models were Sumerian gardens, in which a cultivated patch and its adjacent dwelling were enclosed by protective walls. "Both the garden and the enclosure were aligned with the house and became architectural elements," she explains. "In addition, there was direct access from the house to the garden, which usually consisted of a square or rectangle divided into four beds by two intersecting walkways." She points out that the Sumerians had already espoused the notion of dividing a garden into "rooms."

Another practice that has been in continuous use since this early date is the modification of sloping land by means of retaining walls. Farmers have always terraced their hillsides, but a glamorous application of the technique resulted in the fabled Hanging Gardens of Babylon, which purportedly consisted of seven terraces of diminishing size. The walls supported ascending levels planted with trees. Irrigation for the gardens was provided in some ingenious way by water drawn from the Euphrates River.

The sine qua non of gardening in all hot climates was the diversion of life-sustaining water from river to storage pool. Egyptian tomb paintings show that the decorative possibilities of these utilitarian pools were not overlooked. Reservoirs became the centerpieces of elegantly arranged formal gardens boasting shady grape arbors and trees — palm, fig, and pomegranate — planted to provide protection from the fierce sun as well as for their fruit.

Shade, water, enclosure, and the arrangement of garden features at right angles to a main linear axis — these are the stuff gardens have been made of for thousands of years. As Ragna notes, "The Romans were instrumental in bringing these design concepts to Europe, but so were the Arabs. Ideas traveled with them along the coast of Africa and across to Spain and Italy. It was the Italians who were the catalysts. They absorbed concepts from different cultures, synthesizing them so that they would work for European society. These ideas caught on. In Europe, gardens with long vistas and geometric patterns were done on a grand scale by the aristocracy. I've taken those ideas and scaled them down to a very small area. But I have done it in such a way that it gives you the illusion of space."

It is strange to think that design themes from an ancient, sweltering land in the Middle East should give rise to a modern North American garden that is attractive in all seasons and uniquely beautiful in winter. This garden is in fact made up of three discrete but interlocking gardens, each connected to the others and to the house by walls and fences, walkways and hedges, trellises and arbors. Each garden has its own centerpiece — a stone ornament, a sundial, or a fountain. When the structures and the plantings are crisply outlined in snow, Ragna herself finds the garden a magical place.

Details can be better appreciated in the absence of line-blurring verdure. In the winter, you can enjoy the precise elegance of the trellises and their graceful archways. You might even notice that the openings on the face of the trellises are not square but form horizontal rectangles, which makes the structures seem lighter and lower. If you are extremely observant, you might discover that inside the archways, the rectangular openings have been reversed and are vertical.

Ragna, who worked out these proportions with great care, explains the underlying principle: "Looking through the arches, your eye orients itself on this new, narrower shape and perceives it as a reduction, thus forcing the perspective." Another subtle manipulation of space makes the arches overhead seem higher than they really are. Instead of using a simple semicircular curve, Ragna has raised the height by an additional inch. "Just that little inch makes it seem as if the arch is going upward rather than weighing down the trellis," she points out.

To me, the design of this garden — in plan and in elevation — is like a complex, satisfying puzzle, the kind that you take apart at your peril. But to its creator, devising the plan was easy. At the time the Goddards bought the Cape-style house, it sat on a knoll, presiding over sloping, overgrown fields. There was a grape arbor some distance away, but Ragna saw at once that it had a pleasing relationship to the building, repeating the north-south axis of the roofline. She determined that the garden should connect this structure to the house.

The next step was not easy. The would-be gardener made a discovery that has confounded generations of Connecticut farmers: the soil was root-ridden and almost impenetrable, and soggy, to boot. "That's when I found someone with a plow," Ragna remembers, "but this gentleman only lasted two minutes. He said his equipment was sinking. I said, 'But I must have a garden here. Isn't there anything I can do?' He looked at me and shrugged. 'Well, you could dig a drainage ditch.' I tried to find someone who would dig, but it's not very glamorous or high-paying work, so I had to do the job myself."

Once the drainage ditch was in, Ragna began to make progress. Centering on the grape arbor, she laid out the ground plan with string and stakes. There were to be walks, which she intended to pave with flat stones. However, her husband wanted the stones for a retaining wall. So they made a deal: he could have the stones if he would finance the purchase of old bricks for the walkways. Ragna personally laid between 16,000 and 18,000 bricks. "More than once," she admits ruefully. "I learned there is a certain way of laying bricks and a certain way of *not* laying bricks, and you only find out when you make a mistake."

Once properly laid brick paths divided the fifty-by-one-hundred-foot space and encircled a decorative stone column, Ragna added low boxwood hedges, herbs, and silver foliage plants. Then she turned her attention to the next project. Taking the center axis of the finished garden, she drew a line from south to north. Then she struck another from the middle of the house due west until it intersected with the first line. Where the two lines crossed, she marked the center of a new garden. "Because the house is elevated, only one specific garden was suitable for this location, and that was a knot garden, which ties in with the eighteenth-century style of the house," she explains. Traditionally, a knot garden is planted in an intricate pattern. It is meant to be looked down upon. This garden of overlapping circles within a square is particularly effective when the plants outlining its Persian rug motif are frosted with snow.

Because the area between the knot garden and the brick-paved main garden was open, Ragna chose a covered walkway as the link. "In order to really enjoy gardens, there has to be an even measure of open area and shade," she says. "And there are two ways of creating shade. You can use a manmade structure, or you can take nature itself and create architecture with it." Opting for the second method, she planted six matching trees — old-fashioned Seckel pears — on either side of the walk, drew their supple young branches together, and interwove them overhead.

Meanwhile, Tom had built stone retaining walls to form a secure level platform for the house. It no longer perched on a slope but sat firmly on its site overlooking the property. The two existing gardens were related visually and structurally to the house by fences, hedges, and walkways. But one section still did not please the garden-maker. Ragna kept looking at a flat area between the grape arbor and the house. Finally, it came to her: "I decided there should be a classic garden called the four-fold pattern, with a fountain in the middle."

First she laid out the beds and walkways, and then she set to work with spade and wheelbarrow. Coming upon this busy scene, her son watched for a while, bemused. Finally he shook his head. "You already have two gardens," he said. "And look how many weeds there are. Why are you building another?" To which his mother replied firmly, "Weeds will always be with us, but I have to have another garden right here." It completed the overall design by filling the empty southeast corner of the developed property. The house occupied one corner, the main garden with its brick walks and sundial another — diagonally across from the house — while a generous square of lawn with the knot garden in the middle held down the northwest corner. The fountain garden was as necessary as it was inevitable. Medieval in feeling, it fitted into the fourth quarter of the grounds and was divided into four beds — the magic number in Ragna's gardens. Moreover, it supplied the heretofore missing component — water.

The fountain is an ingenious arrangement of commercially available elements. Ragna bought simple concrete garden benches and laid the tops on edge lengthwise to form the sides of an octagonal basin. From the center, two more shallow basins in graduated sizes rise on pedestals and terminate in a decorative finial. Water shoots up in a jet before tumbling down the tier of basins and being recycled. Cloistered by the grape arbor on one side, a trellis on another, and retaining walls on the remaining two sides, the fountain garden serves as a peaceful retreat in summer. In winter the fountain has to be drained, but its architectural presence enlivens the view from the kitchen window.

Visitors to the Goddard garden — and there are many — receive a little "Guide for Viewing the Gardens." Sites are marked with numbers to orient the onlooker and capitalize on the artfully conceived tableaux. Ragna points out, "Standing by the house, you look down and across the knot garden, through an arched trellis to a birch forest with a statue. If you walk down the steps to the knot garden and stand behind the sundial, looking toward the main garden, you not only look from one garden into the next, you look *through* the pear arbor, and this gives you a marvelous contrast of light and dark areas, of greens and silver. It also gives you the illusion of great depth. Then, standing in the main garden by the sundial and looking through the grape arbor towards the fountain, you are aware that the sundial and fountain are aligned. So it gives you this feeling of allées, of depth, and of vista. These are among the most ancient of all gardening concepts, and they are the essence of this garden."

In winter, when most of the visitors are gone, the gardens are as beautiful as ever. Because they are an extension of the house, the Goddards never feel closed in. There is something that draws the eye from each window beyond the confines of the house and out into the peaceful, orderly landscape, now a study in black and white and shades of gray.

Jack and June Dunbar

A few weeks ago, I discovered that Jack and June Dunbar had put their lovely turn-of-the-century New York City townhouse on the market. It is one of fourteen, all by the same builder and all alike, except that theirs is the last on the east end and the floor plan is the reverse of the others. This has the advantage of providing a few extra feet of garden space, which is why the Dunbars bought it. They have lived and gardened here for twenty-two years. But as I write, Jack is already drawing up plans for a new garden on the country property they have just acquired in Litchfield County, Connecticut.

By the time this book is in print, that garden will be in progress on ten rural acres. It will be as beautiful as the Manhattan one, though a totally different sort of garden. But I am assailed by pangs of regret for what the Dunbars are leaving behind. Soon the glorious weeping beech will belong to strangers. The old grapevine that Jack lovingly pruned for its winter aspect will be neglected. And the climbing rose will run rampant instead of tracing an openwork pattern on the wooden fence.

As a gardener, soft-spoken, gentle Jack Dunbar is a wolf in sheep's clothing. The outward, visible signs in his city garden are of order and restraint. But beneath this sweet reasonableness lies the soul of a craving, covetous plant collector. Only his skill as a pruner and a staker make the garden's perfection possible. The limitations of space and the severe rigidity of the boundary walls and buildings fired his imagination in terms of plant treatment and design.

In a press release for an exhibit of Jack's drawings and paintings, there was a perceptive reference to his garden: "Not surprisingly, his favorite subjects are the fruits, vegetables, and flowers that he cultivates with passionate precision in the city garden behind his Manhattan townhouse." "Passionate precision" is the key to this garden. The separate elements — square sections of wooden decking, planting beds, and plant material — interact like the workings of a watch.

Jack says that he started by putting a grid on paper, because that was an easy way to plan. "The space was thirty feet by thirty-five feet, and the five-foot-square units evolved as I was sitting at the drawing board," he explains. "Of course, I had been working on modular-plan buildings at Skidmore, Owings and Merrill for years, so it was a natural way for me to think about dividing space."

Winter unlocks the secrets of Jack's garden, revealing the zigzag pattern of the decking. The individual units thrust this way and that, as if in search of more space. A skeletal outdoor staircase uncoils to meet the largest platform, which runs the width of the back yard, joining the Dunbars' house to that of their neighbors, the Kleins.

The Dunbars' relationship with the Kleins has been very rewarding. Although Jack designed the garden and the Dunbars have always been the gardeners, it was Arvid Klein, an architect, who actually built the platforms, using the Dunbars' ground-floor apartment as a workshop. Of their joint endeavor, Jack says, "We have always agreed to agree." The result is a garden that has given pleasure to both households.

On the day of my last visit, I stood with Jack at the door of the Kleins' bedroom and surveyed the garden. Because Jack considered this the primary vista, he did many of the preliminary drawings from here. A narrow boardwalk leads out to the main platform. By planting shrubs and perennials very close to the walk and avoiding any species with large leaves, Jack made the distance seem greater and the journey more interesting.

Recently trees were removed from back yards to the south of the garden, letting in additional sunlight, and I noticed last summer that Jack was growing more flowering perennials than I remembered from earlier visits. He had arranged a garden of daylilies in two-gallon pots in the middle of the main platform and suspended hanging baskets of miniature roses, lobelia, helichrysum, and brachycome from the spiral staircase. But in the Dunbar lexicon, colorful flowers are secondary. The emphasis is on handsome, largely evergreen foliage, which gives this garden its strength in the winter.

Nevertheless, Jack has always prided himself on having something in bloom every day of the year. Camellias begin to flower in November and carry on into January, when witch hazel (*Hamamelis* × *intermedia* 'Diana') unfurls wispy red petals from buds that look like peppercorns. Despite the cold, the blossoms last for weeks. Winter jasmine (*Jasminum nudiflorum*) flowers intermittently all winter. Even during the winter of 1993–1994, which produced unheard-of minimum temperatures, the jasmine valiantly put forth a shower of yellow stars along its graceful dark green branches.

Jack usually put potted forget-me-nots in the ground in November for early spring bloom, along with pansies. He claims that the pansies were the reason he and June never went away at Christmastime. "We would go out the day after Christmas and scavenge Christmas trees — that's why we had to be here for the holidays, to cut up the leftover Christmas trees. We would make little houses for the pansies. It looked like a Japanese garden in winter because we did it carefully, so that it was all very designy." They used larger fir branches to shelter the tender camellias and mulched the rest of the garden with buckwheat hulls, whose fine texture and dark brown color set off the plants and manmade evergreen structures.

While new owners of the property will not find pansies and forget-me-nots in the spring, they will be surprised and delighted by the little bulbs that pop up everywhere from January to April. "The garden is full of bulbs," says Jack. "You have this layering business of stuff on top of stuff." He was inspired by a garden in Oxford, England, that was a hundred feet deep but only twenty-five feet wide and that the owner had jammed with plants. "I would never want to have that kind of a garden," he says, "but it gave me the guts to go ahead and lay on more stuff." In a recent search for more room, Jack converted a tiny space against the west wall into a six-inch-wide nursery bed and the home for a new clematis, one of twenty different cultivars that scale the black netting attached to wall and fence. Even in this tight spot, he managed to squeeze in a red-stemmed *Cornus stolonifera* for winter color.

If the new owners fail to appreciate the skill, daring, and work that went into this urban oasis, they will at least admire the great variety of well-deployed evergreens that make the beds seem lush all year long. June Dunbar remembers the painstaking research that went into their selection: "You don't plunge in unless you have done your homework. What has been fascinating has been the slow accumulation of horticultural know-how. You have to find out what can withstand this zone 7 climate and where you can get the plants you want. Obviously, there was a good deal of trial and error, but you become more and more sophisticated along the way."

If people who regard winter as the bleak season buy this house and garden, they will think they have died and gone to heaven. From the deck off the kitchen, they will look down upon the glittering deep green foliage of cherry laurel (*Prunus laurocerasus*), the burnished oval leaves of the camellias, and, at ground level, mounds of handsome palmate leaves belonging to the hellebores. In this sheltered spot, the hellebore foliage remains fresh-looking until spring.

When the Dunbars went out to get the evergreens to form the backbone of the garden, they had a very clear idea of what they wanted and where they wanted to put it. "It really had to do with the ups and downs and the shapes against the fence and the shapes against the wall," says Jack. They chose an evergreen yew for the southwest corner, and evergreen azaleas, rhododendrons, and hollies for along the wall.

In his ongoing quest for more planting area, Jack made the hollies into standards, shrubs trained to a single stem with all the growth confined to a terminal crown of foliage. June describes this metamorphosis: "When we first got the hollies — 'Blue Prince', 'Blue Princess', and the 'Blue Maids' — they were all pyramidal. But Jack said, 'Hey, this is crazy. I can grow all kinds of things underneath them if I remove the lower branches,' which he did." He is a wonderful pruner. He has to be, to keep all the shrubs within bounds. "I have never hesitated to lop anything off at any time," he says.

To maintain order among the perennials, both Dunbars rise early in the summer to remove spent flowers daily. Their gardening has always been a joint effort. They began with houseplants and pots of bulbs in a Greenwich Village apartment. Over the years the rooms became fuller and fuller of more and more plants, particularly more freesias and tulips for the winter. Laughing, June remarks that they were very, very successful at forcing bulbs. After potting, bulbs require a period of cold storage, a condition easily met in the Dunbars' unheated apartment. With the arrival of warm weather, they moved their activities up to the roof and gardened there in boxes — until the roof began to leak.

Eventually they were able to indulge their passion and hone their skills in Northampton County, Pennsylvania, where for a few years they owned an old stone farmhouse. But their gardening education really began soon after they were married. June remembers their mentor with gratitude: "An enormously influential person in our gardening lives was Gertrude Thayer Almy. Mr. and Mrs. Almy were the parents of one of my college roommates. They lived about thirty miles west of Philadelphia, and we saw a lot of them before we had our house. Mrs. Almy was a passionate, knowledgeable gardener. She grew all of her own annuals and biennials, and some perennials from seed. And she insisted on calling all plants by their Latin names. We learned a tremendous amount from her and had fun helping in her garden."

Both Jack and June also had fathers who enjoyed gardening and who passed this interest on to their offspring. Jack pinpoints his third-grade year as the beginning of his gardening career. "That year," he explains, "the Cleveland public school system organized a program providing vegetable seeds and three tomato plants for a five-by-fifteen-foot garden — all for fifty cents. It took a lot of convincing to persuade my father to dig up a piece of his lawn for this vegetable garden, but he did. And for four summers I had my garden. Every year my homeroom teacher would come twice during the summer to check on my progress. After that, I was allowed to help in my father's garden."

June remembers helping her father in his garden when they had a house in Vermont in the summertime. "I think I was the only one of the five of us who enjoyed being down there working with him. I loved weeding," she says. She still is the weeder. "Jack has always been the conceptualizer of the garden, and I have always been the helper. I have ideas and put in my two cents when I feel strongly about where something should be, but he is in charge of the grand design."

I was fascinated to discover that Jack arrived at design as a vocation and avocation by a circuitous route that included very little formal training. As he tells it, "I spent a semester at the Cleveland School of Art before I was drafted into the army during the Second World War. After the army, I had two months as an apprentice at Taliesin, the summer home of Frank Lloyd Wright. There were sixty apprentices, all learning to do architecture, and I convinced myself that I could become an architect if I went there."

He didn't become an architect, but he did meet June, who was at Taliesin to attend her sister's wedding. And he furthered his gardening education. "What I absolutely loved about the place was the land, the farm and the gardens," Jack says. "Part of one's duty was working in the gardens every day, and I really loved doing it. It was one of my favorite things about the whole experience."

After that he fumbled around for a bit, traveled in Europe on the proverbial shoestring, and finally, having ascertained that June was in town, descended on New York City with $72 in his pocket. June, then a dancer, was also penniless, but she says that she was never nervous about their finances. Young, talented, and supremely confident, they soon married.

Jack had discovered photography during his travels abroad and arrived in New York with a portfolio. He trotted it around to magazine art directors and got a job as an assistant to architectural photographer Ezra Stoller. "He hired me in the morning, and in the afternoon we got on a plane to Cincinnati to photograph the Terrace Plaza Hotel, which, as it turned out, was a Skidmore, Owings and Merrill building," Jack remembers.

To make a long story short, he eventually wound up at Skidmore, Owings and Merrill as head of the new interior design department. At thirty-one, he found himself responsible for the Union Carbide Building, designing everything from ashtrays to wallpaper to floor coverings. But in a distinguished career as a designer, nothing has given him more satisfaction than planning and working in his own gardens.

"I was always nurturing the artist and worrying about when he was going to get going," he says. "Here in the garden, it all came together. The designer put the framework together — there was no question in my mind that I knew what I was doing. And then the artist got busy with this color and form thing." The result is a memorable garden.

The camellias that Jack and June planted will bloom for a different audience this year, and without its vigilant pruner, the garden will change. The Kleins, devastated by the departure of their neighbors, may install the decorative fence Jack has designed to divide the two gardens once again, or perhaps they will forge an alliance with their new neighbors. Whatever else happens, when next winter comes, Jack Dunbar will be at the drawing board, fine-tuning the design for the new garden.

Planned and Planted for the Birds

To make a garden is to create a habitat for birds. Birds need food, shelter, and water, and gardens supply these necessities. Even the smallest suburban garden provides staples in the form of seeds and berries. The ubiquitous junipers, yews, azaleas, and rhododendrons used for foundation plantings offer sanctuary. Birds also love protective tangles of forsythia and other common deciduous shrubs.

In return for these safe havens and a reliable source of food and water during the winter, they become year-round residents and useful allies. In the summer, they consume thousands of aphids, flying insects, and caterpillars. In order to feed themselves and their broods, they perform miracles. In one documented case, a pair of titmice fed their nine young on insects at an average rate of thirty-three times a day.

In the winter, titmice, which are thought to remain in a given place year after year, are among the most engaging visitors to our birdfeeder. Trimly turned out in dark and light gray, with a jaunty crest and large, bright black eyes, they display the restless, frantic flight pattern associated with insect hunters. When the insect supply dwindles with the onset of cold weather, they make do with the sunflower seeds we provide. Mounting quick rushes at the feeder, they snatch up a seed, then repair to a nearby maple to eat it in peace.

Our birdfeeder is set on a metal pole outside the kitchen window, where we can observe these delightful comings and goings. Shy of humans, the titmice object if I go too close to the sink beneath the window. They are even touchy about sharing the perch with other birds. When they are interrupted at the feeder, they flatten their crests and charge at the interloper.

The chickadees, in contrast, are amiable and outgoing. Of all the winter birds, these tiny, game little creatures are my favorites. I love their faces, masked with an hourglass of black, and their eyes, like minuscule jet beads. By far the friendliest of the birds, they are always hanging around the back door. They perch in a conveniently located viburnum. Sometimes there will be half a dozen of them among the bare twigs, awaiting a place at the feeder.

What has been a revelation to us this winter is the importance of providing them with water. A year ago I visited a gardening friend whose terrace was alive with birds. They were flocking not to the well-stocked feeders but to the shallow containers of water she had provided. She had installed electric heating elements in the birdbaths to prevent ice from forming, and the numbers of birds availing themselves of the water amazed me.

On the strength of that experience, we acquired a heated birdbath, which has been a delight to us and a much appreciated source of fresh water to the birds. It has also given rise to great hilarity among our city-dwelling friends, who imagine the chickadees and juncos disporting themselves in some sort of hot tub. Their mirth notwithstanding, the heated birdbath was a worthwhile purchase and has given us hours of bird-watching pleasure.

I am still deeply envious of my pen friends Mary and Dick Kordes, in Michigan, who have a flock of tame chickadees. Mary writes: "Our chickadees have truly enriched our winter lives. They follow us whenever we leave the house, chattering and flying to us to be hand-fed. We must never leave the house without sunflower seeds in our pockets or we'll have disappointed birds and a guilty conscience. If Dick is out pruning, I often see him stop sawing to dig in his pocket and hold out a handful of seed. The chickadees swarm around him, sitting on his head and arms as they wait their turn at his hand."

In one letter, Mary recounted how one day last spring Dick felt a chickadee land on his cap and heard the sound of its nails tap-tapping on the stiff brim. The next thing he knew, the chickadee was hanging upside down from the peak, looking him in the eye. That story inspired me to stand motionless for hours near our birdfeeder, sunflower seed in hand. But the chickadees invariably bypassed my outstretched palm on their way to the more familiar source.

Every gardener interviewed for this book regards bird-watching as one of winter's keenest pleasures. All of us are grateful to these small creatures for bringing sound, motion, and color to the frozen landscape. They dart, skim, swoop, and flit among the leafless trees — eastern bluebirds, like scraps of cobalt confetti; dapper gray juncos; many kinds of sparrows, streaked here and there with a bit of white or yellow or chestnut; noisy, quarrelsome purple finches, the color of crushed raspberries; and handsome red cardinals with chic, olive-clad wives.

Most of my gardening friends have birdfeeders and do what they can to attract these remarkable wild creatures, but Christine Utterback of New Hartford, Connecticut, has gone a step further. She commissioned Mary Ann McGourty of Hillside Gardens in Norfolk to design a garden especially for the birds.

Christine Utterback

"Admittedly, attracting birds has been easy for us," Christine Utterback wrote in the Connecticut Horticultural Society newsletter. "We live in an area surrounded by woods, with numerous nesting sites, food, and water sources already in place. Native plants such as brambles, impatiens (jewel-weed), grapes, thistles, amaranth, lamb's quarters, even oak, mountain ash, and pine trees, all provide food for birds during different times of the year. An herbal tree, *Rhus typhina* (staghorn sumac), edging our property has attracted hairy woodpeckers, and even a flock of robins caught in a late spring snowstorm."

The Utterbacks' bird garden was intended to add new food sources and to enhance the property, and Mary Ann McGourty's design succeeds in both respects. Chris wanted something that would blend into the surrounding landscape. "Because our house is made of logs and because we live in a rural area," she explains, "we wanted a garden that wasn't too fussy or formal. We wanted plants that would make a transition from the wild stuff in the woods to the cultivated things in the yard without a big contrast. I think Mary Ann did a wonderful job. She picked plants that are similar to the things that grow here naturally. We already have viburnums, ilex, and the grasses across the road in the meadow. I'm amazed that more gardeners don't use ornamental grasses. We get a lot of comments about them from people walking by."

The Utterbacks live on an unpaved road in the valley that lies between the Barkhamsted and Nepaug reservoirs. Foot traffic is more common than cars. Across the road that runs parallel to their house, meadows and cornfields stretch toward the wooded hills. The land is federal floodplain and therefore protected from development. This lovely pastoral scene is the backdrop for the bird garden.

To preserve the view from the house, Mary Ann McGourty chose a compact form of burning bush (*Euonymus alatus* 'Compactus') to make an unpruned hedge between the front lawn and the road. The hedge is backed by seventy feet of split rail fence, now weathered to a soft shade of silver-gray. Shorter sections of fence placed at right angles to the boundary fence partially enclose the front lawn and create corners for tall plantings of winterberry, barberry, and American cranberry bush (*Viburnum trilobum*). All produce bird-pleasing crops, the showiest of which are the viburnum's dangling clusters of large, glassy red fruits, each one a third of an inch across.

In the winter this garden is as appealing to the human eye as it is attractive to the birds. The euonymus, which has interesting ridged bark and a fan-shaped branching pattern, is also hung with dainty red capsules that split open to reveal orange-coated seeds. The berried shrubs at either end are interplanted with golden grasses, intensely blue *Juniperus squamata* 'Blue Star', brown, bushy *Spiraea* × *bumalda* 'Anthony Waterer', and low mounds of fine-twigged *S. japonica* var. *alpina*. Both spiraeas have flat, papery flower heads that catch the snow.

The living room windows overlook the bird garden and the view beyond. Inside, the house has a southwestern flavor, with wide floorboards and wood everywhere. There are colorful rugs on the walls and comfortable mission-style furniture. The old desk in one corner looks like a still life with its cozy clutter of decorative birdhouses, bird nests, stacks of bird books, and a pair of Navy surplus binoculars. But it is also a working desk where Chris spends a lot of time. She is, among other things, a free-lance writer.

Above the desk, bunches of dried herbs hang from the ceiling. A knowledgeable herb grower and the editor of her own newsletter, a stylish, attractive publication called *Herban Lifestyles,* Chris is modest and funny when it comes to discussing her many winter enthusiasms, which include crafts of all kinds.

One year she got a glue gun and didn't emerge from the basement for weeks. When she did surface, she had made beautiful Christmas package decorations with paper ribbon and dried herbs, pods, pine cones, and sunflowers from the garden. She chuckled when I asked about her ongoing interests and said, "I change all the time. I usually do something for Christmas, though — make a big arrangement, make potpourri. I mean to do things with dried herbs, but what usually happens is that I hang them up with an elastic band. Eventually the rubber band breaks, they fall on the floor, and I either put them in a vase or throw them out."

The thread connecting her many activities is a love of gardening, which began in a back yard in Clearwater, Florida, with a father who enjoyed "puttering around outside." Her involvement with herbs developed much later, when she found herself living in Denver in a house with an attached greenhouse. "I was growing all this tarragon, and I had much more than I could use, so I sold it to some of the really nice restaurants in Denver," she explains. On the strength of these sales, she quit her job as head nurse for a physician and went into the herb business. That spawned *Herban Lifestyles*.

Three months after launching the newsletter, Chris and her husband, Bob, whose work brought them to Connecticut, found their present house and settled in. They love their adopted state and the log house with its two rural acres. *Herban Lifestyles* survived the move, and now, instead of being devoted to high-altitude herb growing, it contains all kinds of ideas about herb gardening and related activities.

Chris does everything with the newsletter except print it. I asked how she acquired her typesetting and graphic skills. "I kind of fell into it," she says. "Out in Denver, we had a homeowners' association, and we put out an association newsletter. I was on the board and somehow ended up doing the newsletter. The woman I replaced was a typesetter by profession, and she taught me how to do it." She is rightly proud of the appearance of her newsletter and tries to make the content equally attractive and unusual.

"There are lots of things related to herb gardening," she says. "I've got cooking, I've got birds, I've got basketry, I've got health and the environment." One of her favorite issues has an extended article on how and where to collect gardening books; another favorite discusses the pleasures of friendship and the ceremony of tea.

She particularly likes putting together the winter issues. "I urge people to woolgather, to think about the whole cycle of death and rebirth, and to rest up for spring. I love winter. The garden has enough structure so it always looks like a garden. We have a lot of wildlife. I enjoy that in the winter. I looked out one day, and there was a red fox with black feet, standing in the snow. It was just such a gorgeous sight."

The first time Chris saw a pileated woodpecker, she was so excited that she called her husband at work and said, "I've just seen a red-headed pterodactyl!" The Utterbacks have birdfeeders on every side of the house. The kitchen opens eastward onto a deck built into a steep, rocky, hemlock-covered hillside. In the winter, birds shelter in the evergreens and come to the deck feeder. On the west is Mary Ann's shrub border with its rich smorgasbord of birdfood, and close to the house, a crab-apple tree attracts many avian visitors. Chris described the descent of a flock of evening grosbeaks: "One year they came through and stripped the tree before continuing on their way. We also have grouse, all kinds of hawks, bluejays, chickadees, juncos, cardinals, titmice, and both downy and hairy woodpeckers, who come for the suet. My goal in life is to have a chickadee eat out of my hand. I think I really wanted to be Saint Francis."

Extending the Season

In the fall, I find myself beset by conflicting emotions. If the growing season has been kind, I can hardly bear to see it end. The glorious English-style summer of 1992 was my idea of heaven — rain, rain, rain. The plants loved it, and so did I. The garden looked as I imagine it only in my wildest dreams. That year, it made me weep to see the leaves drop. But the end of the following summer couldn't come soon enough. Devastating drought and a plague of moles left me longing for a blanket of snow to hide the whole miserable business.

In the average season, there are enough triumphs to balance the disasters, and I feel torn between relief and sadness — sadness because the garden will never be quite the same again; relief for the same reason. There will be new highs and new lows, but never those that have just been. On the plus side, the battle is over. For the self-employed garden writer, a great struggle ceases with the onset of winter. There is no longer that wrenching choice between writing and gardening.

I like looking down from my office window on the winter-ready garden. The edging of lamb's ears looks like a flat silver ribbon defining the perennial border. The ugly, mushy foliage of the daylilies has been cleaned up, and the only perennials left standing are the staples of the winter garden: grasses, shrubs, *Sedum* 'Autumn Joy', and *Calamintha nepeta nepeta,* which leaves a puff of interlacing stems as fine as threads.

When the border is tidy and the leaves have been raked, chopped, and collected behind the barn, when the clay pots are under cover and the pump has been disconnected and stored in the cellar, I am more than content to see the snow fly. Roll on, winter! The landscape is spare and restful, and the garden calm. No plant cries out for water; no teetering stem demands a stake. The woodchuck has retired to his burrow up in the field, and no beetle munches.

There are plenty of things I could do outside if I wanted to, but mostly I don't. I can write in peace. And I have more time to read or just sit at the kitchen table, looking through the sliding glass doors. Maybe it's laziness or old age or both, but to me, winter is for rest and repose.

Now, the gardeners in the next chapters do not hold with this view of winter. They don't want the growing season to end. And they don't want to stop gardening. Doing, not being, is their first joy. Whether you choose to join them or prefer to observe their activities from afar, you have to admire them. These stalwart souls have, in their different ways, succeeded in prolonging the garden year.

Barbara Damrosch and Eliot Coleman

A winter meal with Barbara Damrosch and her husband, Eliot Coleman, in Harborside, Maine, would tell you immediately why they belong in this book. Imagine a bowl of smooth squash soup at your place, and a crisp salad of curly endive combined with small green rosettes of mache and a few shocking-pink leaves of radicchio. The next course could be roasted beets, to match the radicchio, served with pale julienne sticks of celeriac or puréed root vegetables. In case you couldn't wait for the main course, you could try some raw carrots, as sweet as honey, from a bowl on the long trestle table. Not only is the food at their house wonderful all winter long, it all comes straight from the garden — a garden often engulfed by deep snow.

This bountiful harvest is made possible by the ingenuity and determination of your host. Eliot has devised a means of using cold frames within a plastic-covered hoop house to lull cold-tolerant vegetables into near-dormancy and to keep them in perfect condition for two months or more. Vegetables sown in the early fall continue growing until mid-November beneath the two layers of protection. When growth stops, they mark time, waiting for spring. Beginning in mid-January, Eliot starts sowing spring crops in any empty spots. "All this system is doing," he insists, "is holding the produce. The great thing is that we're doing six months of free harvesting. Basically, we have two major planting seasons, spring and early fall, and the rest of the time it's just eating."

In his book *The Four-Season Harvest,* he shares his methods in detail, assuring home gardeners that they too can enjoy the benefits of fresh vegetables all year. His tunnel greenhouse measures seventeen feet wide by thirty-two feet long, which he admits is large. Not everyone would want or need such a commodious structure. However, it is all homemade and not beyond the skills of the average handyman or homeowner.

Eliot is convinced that if more people knew about these low-cost tunnel greenhouses, no home would be without one. "One layer of protection, either the cold frame alone or the greenhouse by itself, moves you a zone and a half to the south," he points out. "And the second layer moves you another zone and a half to the south. So you walk into the greenhouse, and you're in New Jersey. You reach your hand into the cold frame, and you're in Georgia. It's as simple as that."

An important aspect of this system is its mobility. Based on European models, the greenhouse sits on wooden rails twice its own length, thus providing two sites for planting. In position one, the tunnel covers the cold frames planted with the winter harvest. In the spring, when these crops are played out, they are replaced by hot-weather crops like tomatoes and peppers. After the hot-weather crops have been harvested, the tunnel remains empty. Meanwhile, the cold frames in position two are planted with a new winter harvest. In October, the tunnel is moved along its rails to position two, so it covers the summer-sown crops. Every time the tunnel is moved to the alternate position, a section of the garden lies uncovered and exposed to the elements for a season, thereby avoiding any buildup of pests or diseases.

Barbara explains that Eliot is always starting things, harvesting things, or replanting things. "That way, it isn't so labor-intensive at any one point during the year. Growing your own food really isn't that much work. The food sort of gets taken care of the way you do your housework."

Although she and Eliot could take time off during the winter, relaxing and eating like kings, they choose to do otherwise. This winter they will be working on a book together and possibly developing a new television series on gardening. Their first, called *Gardening Naturally*, is already in reruns. In the meantime, Eliot has been closeted in his office revising his first book, *The New Organic Grower: A Master's Manual of Tools and Techniques for the Home and Market Gardener*. In an adjoining office, Barbara, who is the author of *Theme Gardens* and *The Garden Primer*, has just finished her sixth Gardener's Page-a-Day Calendar for Workman Press.

When they are not at their desks or gathering fresh vegetables from the garden, they are energetically occupied outdoors. If there is snow, Barbara sets forth on cross-country skis, while Eliot plays ice hockey on a nearby pond. What he and his neighbors actually play is a European game called bandy. Bandy employs a little ball instead of a puck, and the sticks are similar to field hockey sticks. There is a game every afternoon at three o'clock, and any number can join in. Sometimes there are as few as four; on other occasions, as many as fifteen or sixteen. "But the craziest thing is our sauna," says Barbara. "Talk about unusual ways to spend the winter!"

Many of the neighbors also have saunas, and sweating together is a popular social activity. The heat provided by a woodstove soars to two hundred degrees and at some point drives participants outdoors to roll in the snow or jump into a body of frigid water. "When you start to actually feel cold, you go back inside for more," Barbara explains. "And by the time you get out of there, you feel like a million dollars." I'm afraid I remain unconvinced.

Barbara and Eliot have only recently combined their formidable energies and talents. But even before they met, four years ago, they had a lot in common. They both come from comfortable urban or suburban back-grounds — she grew up in New York City; his home was in New Jersey. Each had a degree in literature — hers in medieval literature, his in Spanish literature. And they had both been teachers. All quite ordinary. What was out of the ordinary was a shared dream of living off the land somewhere far from the madding crowd.

When I try to describe their life together, verbs expressing vigorous athleticism immediately come to mind, phrases like "teaming up" or "joining forces." Forces they certainly are, individually and collectively. Eliot refers to their alliance as a merger. But if this relationship is a merger, it is one in which each individual retains complete autonomy. For twenty years before their paths crossed, each had led a strenuous, workaholic life that included marriage to other partners, raising children, and gaining recognition in their respective fields — Barbara as a garden writer, Eliot in organic farming.

Now in his fifties, Eliot still emanates the restless vitality of a young man on the brink of a great enterprise. To him, the discovery of organic farming was just that. And twenty-five years of following the gleam has not dimin-ished his enthusiasm. A self-described adventurer, he used to teach school so that he could have the summers free to go rock climbing, white-water kayaking, and mountaineering. Then one day he read a book on organic farming. "I said, 'Wow! That sounds like the neatest adventure I've ever heard of!'"

The book was *Living the Good Life,* by Helen and Scott Nearing, which chronicles the design and execution of a lifestyle dependent on the land and on each other. In 1932 the Nearings abandoned city life for Vermont, self-sufficiency, a vegetarian diet, and growing their food without benefit of pesticides or chemical fertilizers. They believed in eating for their own good health and that of the planet. Twenty years later they moved to Harborside, Maine, to carry on their unique brand of rural homesteading.

A decade or so later, young Eliot Coleman found himself teaching at a small college in Franconia, New Hampshire. As the Dartmouth College library was only an hour away, he often ensconced himself in the stacks, and by the end of a year he had worked his way through the subject of agriculture. "I didn't know what I wanted to learn, so I figured I might as well read everything," he says. "The conventional books made farming sound like taking the chairlift to the top of the mountain. But with the organic stuff, there was so much excitement in figuring out how to work with natural systems. That has been a constant fascination ever since."

Instead of overwhelming nature with chemicals, Eliot augments the natural order of things, planting cover crops and adding compost to maintain soil fertility. "I look upon the natural world as this incredible resource of everything the gardener needs, and I try to pay attention so that I can just fit myself into the system and flow with it," he explains.

The short form of Eliot's plunge into organic farming and his first marriage goes like this. He and his wife, Susan, arrived in Maine to visit Helen and Scott Nearing. Convinced by what they saw of the good life, they returned the following year, this time to look for land. Charmed by the young couple's ardor, the Nearings offered them forty acres at a price they could afford — $33 an acre. Eliot and Susan proceeded to clear the trees and build their own house. By the second spring they had enough land under cultivation to begin selling produce, and by the end of the fourth year, they were supporting themselves from the market garden.

This feat is even more miraculous considering their location miles from the nearest habitation. As Eliot explains, "We sold vegetables right here at the farm. People had to drive six miles off the main road, the last three of which were dirt. We used to put a notice in the paper when we opened in the spring, and that was all the advertising we did. Word-of-mouth is what builds businesses, and if you have a good product, everybody is just ecstatic to have it." The Colemans built their reputation by growing dozens of different kinds of vegetables of the highest quality, and the farmstand caught on. So successful was it that a reporter from the *Wall Street Journal* wrote it up, and the article made the front page. It delights Eliot to recall this coup: "They were amazed because a hippy farmer was actually making money."

However, success had a high price. The long hours of physical labor and caring for three small children took their toll on the marriage, which ended in 1978. Eliot then went off and got a job running an experimental organic farm in Massachusetts. His early experiments in extending the season of harvest began at Topsfield. "Back then, the Department of Energy was giving grants for stuff," he says. "We got a DOE grant to investigate no-energy out-of-season production, and what we experimented with was a cold frame design that I'd seen in Holland."

So-called Dutch lights are simple frames made with a single pane of glass. They sit on top of the cold frame "like the cover of a pan." Eliot found that he and his colleagues were able to do a remarkable job of out-of-season production just by using these devices efficiently. One of the crops he discovered during his tenure at Topsfield was "candy carrots." Carrots sowed on the first of August were covered with eight to twelve inches of straw in November and left in the Dutch-style cold frames until February. "When we left them in the cold soil, the same thing happened that happens with parsnips. Some of the starch changed to sugar, and the flavor of these things was just unbelievable," he claims.

There was also a small greenhouse at Topsfield, and one winter Eliot happened to lay cold frame glass over the soil inside. He was surprised to note how much extra warmth there was in the soil under the glass. But it wasn't until he moved on to the Mountain School in Vermont that he tumbled to the technique he has now perfected. The school had for years maintained heated greenhouses where the staff raised tomatoes in the winter. But the eighties brought a financial crunch to independent schools, and the heat was turned off at Thanksgiving. As Eliot explains, "Now I had unheated greenhouses, so I took to planting stuff in the soil in the greenhouse, just to see what would happen." What happened was a revelation. In

Barbara Damrosch and Eliot Coleman stand at the entrance to the hoop house that covers their cold frames.

Barbara emerges with a basket full of fresh garden produce. The red cabbage is from the root cellar, and the carrots are grown in an outdoor cold frame.

Hot, rib-sticking food out of the winter garden: Barbara's own sun-dried tomatoes enliven beans, which she serves with squash soup.

Summer in winter: these fresh salad greens came straight from the February garden.

Opposite: The lids of the cold frames inside the hoop house are propped open for ventilation.

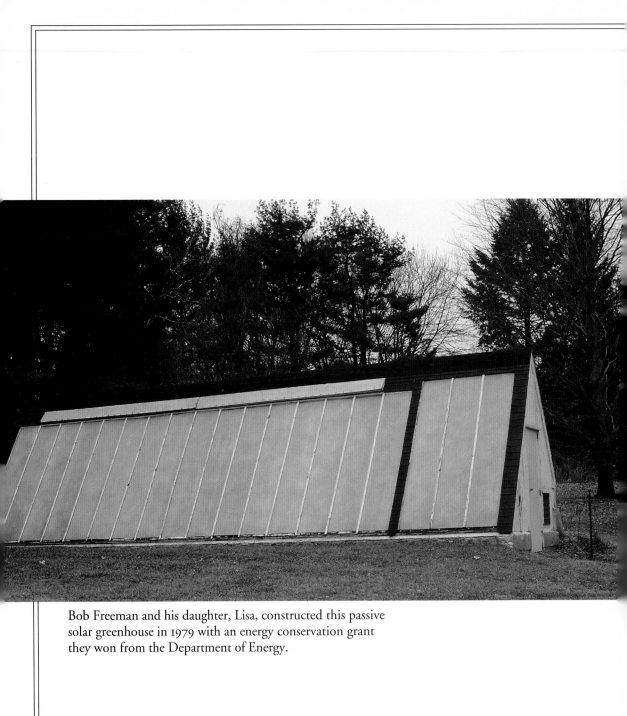

Bob Freeman and his daughter, Lisa, constructed this passive
solar greenhouse in 1979 with an energy conservation grant
they won from the Department of Energy.

In February, jasmine shares bench space with an orange tree and primroses in the Freemans' greenhouse. A wall of five-gallon plastic containers filled with water and painted black collects solar heat during the day and releases it at night, when the temperature drops.

Amaryllis glows against a vibrant yellow background of jasmine.

Opposite: Joan and Avery Larned feed logs to the splitter that they own jointly with neighbors. It takes six or seven cords of wood to fuel the evaporator that boils down the maple sap for their syrup-making business. Avery built the sugarhouse in the background.

Above: Joan removes inner branches of an apple tree in her orchard to admit air and light. The best tool for this job is a pruning saw.

Hugh Davis's replica of a double picket fence he saw in Tewkesbury, England, graces a corner of the garden.

Some of Dick Kordes's handiwork, made from wood grown on the Kordes property: the mallard decoy is carved out of cedar, and the Norwegian bentwood box is made from poplar and decorated with cedar-root "lacing." Dick also taught himself to weave the Nantucket lightship baskets.

that zone 3 climate, where the temperature regularly dipped to forty below zero, he was able to grow many varieties of cold-tolerant vegetables — mache, spinach, Swiss chard, arugula, parsley, perennial garden sorrel, leeks, carrots, and others.

When he returned to Maine in 1990, Eliot began putting into practice all that he had learned from his experiences at Topsfield and the Mountain School. Alongside the present hoop greenhouse, the land is being readied for several much larger greenhouses. Cold frames within are too labor-intensive for commercial production because they have to be vented by hand, but he hopes to compensate for the double layer of protection by using a "night curtain" to reflect the heat built up during the day.

Although he and Barbara may do another gardening show, he still regards appearing on television as a temporary thing. "I'm a farmer," he says. "I'm going back into farming, and I am determined that I can make a living selling produce from September to May and take the summer off — which any civilized individual would want to do."

Barbara, no less than Eliot, was always interested in the back-to-the-land movement. Although she was brought up in New York City, her family had a country house in Connecticut. Her father, a busy pediatrician, used to spend two weekends out of three there. "For him, it was a real retreat. His release was to knock himself out in the garden," Barbara says. But her grandparents' home in Louisiana was "the ultimate paradise" to her as a child: "It was my favorite place in the whole world. They had fabulous gardens, and I just loved it there. So that was part of my heritage."

These memories were always at the back of her mind as life pulled her in different directions. After a youthful marriage failed, she returned to graduate school and taught for several years to support herself and her young son. Next she turned to free-lance magazine writing, but when the lure of country living proved irresistible, she left the city for Washington, Connecticut. "I really wanted to work outdoors and to grow my own food," she explains, "so I went to work at a nursery. That was very successful and led to my designing gardens and writing garden books."

Meanwhile, her parents had moved up to Maine, and in the spring of 1991 her father died. That summer, while Barbara was staying with her mother, a mutual friend from Connecticut arranged for her to meet Helen Nearing, whom she had long admired. "Eliot was there in Helen's greenhouse, tying up her tomatoes. We instantly realized how much we had in common. And I found him so attractive that I was actually willing to give up a month of the growing season to live up here."

Instead of returning to Connecticut after their chance meeting, Barbara stayed on. That was in July. On December 15 of the same year, she and Eliot were married, with only her mother and the neighbors present. The next summer the union was celebrated with "a real hoedown" at the Cape Rosier Grange Hall. This weathered gray wooden structure is a landmark along the circuitous route from the village of Blue Hill to the Damrosch/Coleman establishment.

Barbara was not sorry to leave Connecticut behind. Although she was giving up a thriving landscape design business, she felt that life had become a rat race. Between working, sending her son to college, and trying to make ends meet, she had "kind of lost sight of the dream." She had been thinking seriously of selling her place in Washington to look for land in upstate New York. Then she paid her mother a visit in Maine and rediscovered her direction in Helen Nearing's greenhouse. Living the good life à la Damrosch and Coleman requires energy, ambition, and plain hard work. "But this," says Barbara, "is really what I always wanted to do. So here I am."

Lisa, Bob, and Dodie Freeman

In 1979, Bob Freeman, a middle school mathematics teacher, won one of the thirty federal grants awarded by the Department of Energy to residents of Pennsylvania. It was similar to the grant received by Eliot Coleman to investigate no-energy out-of-season crop production at the experimental farm in Massachusetts. In those days, fear of another oil shortage inspired many creative experiments in energy conservation. Alas, memories are short, and we seem to have returned to our profligate ways, but at that time, interest in finding alternative sources of energy was high.

Bob and his younger daughter, Lisa, had already been working on a small solar greenhouse to extend the growing season. In the summer of 1977, they built a wooden A-frame structure five feet wide, five feet high, and ten feet long and covered it with polyethylene. They chose a site in full sun with a windbreak of evergreens to the north and west. By autumn, the A-frame was ready for action. In eager anticipation, they planted lettuce and parsley and sat back to await their first harvest of fresh salad greens. Then reality set in.

Bob described their experience in an article for the *Green Scene,* the magazine of the Pennsylvania Horticultural Society: "Before the cold weather had progressed very far, we added three sixty-watt light bulbs to boost the temperature on the most frigid nights. The lettuce crop never died out on us, but on the other hand, we weren't overwhelmed with salads either. The second winter we placed a row of plastic milk jugs filled with water and painted black in the back of the structure in the hopes of providing some additional nighttime heat. We didn't notice any appreciable improvement."

Undaunted, they continued to tinker with their A-frame. Then Bob received a notice in the mail about a government-sponsored plan called the Appropriate Energy Technology Small Grants Program. "We had been working on a larger structure and were playing around with that when we learned about this program," he says. "President Carter was trying to involve little people, nonprofessionals, in ways to save energy, so we sent off and got a twenty-six-page booklet to fill out."

Among the forms the Freemans were required to complete was one requesting biographies of "key people who will contribute to the performance of the project." Lisa's name headed the roster. Twenty-six at the time and a graduate of Temple University's Ambler School of Horticulture, she was already a professional gardener with seven years' experience.

Her mother's credits were listed as "housewife; professional flower arranger and decorator; operates family greenhouse; paints." Dodie Freeman is in fact a gifted amateur painter who would like to have studied seriously. "My father and his sisters always drew. We've always been able to, I guess. If I had my life to live over again, I would love to have gone to the Pennsylvania Academy of Fine Arts, instead of diddling around the way I have. You know, girls weren't expected to do much. I'm sorry I didn't, because I would have loved it," she reflects. Alternatively, she would have enjoyed the Ambler School of Horticulture, where Lisa studied, but her own life and accomplishments have given her pleasure and inspired others.

Bob's qualifications for the project included his experience tending their fourteen-acre property, including vegetable garden, orchard, cold frame, and raspberry patch, and his skill as a carpenter. Previously, he had built a substantial addition to their old Pennsylvania farmhouse, as well as a large garage cum workshop with an apartment above it.

When I asked him how he came to know so much about carpentry, he smiled and said, "In seventh grade, I remember, I made a kitchen step-stool, the kind with steps that fold out. Mine worked and my older brother's fell apart. I guess that started me. Then, when Dodie and I had been married for about nine months, we bought this place. We realized that we would have to do things ourselves because we couldn't afford to have them done for us, so I went to Sears, Roebuck and bought seventy-five dollars' worth of the tools I thought I would need." A local carpenter showed him a few tricks of the trade, and Bob was launched.

The Freemans' application for a passive solar greenhouse was duly submitted on April 23, 1979, with a price tag of $5,000. Sometime later, a local representative of the Department of Energy called to say that the list of possible recipients had been narrowed down and the Freemans were still in the running. "They said if we could get the cost down, it would probably make a big difference," Bob explains. "So we did. We resubmitted our price, and a week or so later we won." They were awarded $4,809.

The good news threw them into a flurry of activity. Time was short. The project had to be completed within a year, at which time the public would be invited to view their handiwork. It was already October. Fortunately, temperatures were mild that fall. The shop teacher at Bob's school, who had agreed to dig and pour the foundation, finished it by the end of the month. Bob and Lisa began framing on December first. The weather continued to cooperate, and they completed the job on New Year's Day. During Easter week they installed fiberglass double glazing, and they spent the early summer painting and doing odds and ends. On a very hot weekend in July, they opened their new solar greenhouse to visitors.

Mary Lou Wolfe vividly recalled the day ten years later in an article for the *Green Scene:* "I saw the Freemans' pit structure on a beastly hot July 1980 day when they opened it for a public visit, as specified in the terms of the Department of Energy grant they had received to build it. Along with a hundred other visitors, I signed the guest book, marveled at this compact, bright space, and wondered whether it would really work."

In fact, the Freemans' solar greenhouse has worked like a charm for fourteen years. With no electrical backup system — even the vents are opened and closed by sun-powered heat "motors" — the nighttime temperature has only once gone below forty degrees, and that was during the notorious winter of 1993–1994. "There were no sunny days, and the outdoor temperature got down into the single numbers and even below zero," Bob relates. Normally this part of Pennsylvania is considered zone 7, with average minimum winter temperatures well above zero.

Although Bob designed the structure, he credits the publishers of *Organic Gardening* with practical help and advice. "The Rodale company, up the road in Emmaus, was always interested in the environment and in saving energy," he says. "We went up to see them one day and were shown the various experiments they were trying — not only the buildings, but also what you could grow in them." In addition, Rodale Press had just published *The Solar Greenhouse Book,* edited by James C. McCullagh, and for the next few months that book became the Freemans' bible.

"We learned that the angle of the south-facing roof had to be perpendicular to the sun at its lowest point for the best solar penetration. The angle of the north roof was determined by the height of the stacked water containers," Bob explains. The building is not quite an A-frame, because the lower part of the north wall is vertical to accommodate three hundred five-gallon plastic bottles arranged against it in eight tiers. The bottles are coated with flat black latex paint and filled with water. During the day, the water reaches about sixty degrees. At night the solar heat is released into the atmosphere.

Bob devised a protective night curtain to provide extra insulation against extreme cold. Four panels of inch-thick foam insulation board fold down from the rear roof to cover the interior completely. "Whenever it looks as if it's going to get below fifteen degrees at night, which may be about twenty nights a season, I come down here and lower the panels into place," he says. "They are made of a building material used on the outer wall of a house before they put on the sheathing. It's all foam inside, with a covering of aluminum." Awkward to handle but effective, the rigid panels are supported when not in use by wooden Ts.

By excavating to three feet for the A-frame, Bob incorporated one of the heat-saving features of alpine houses, which are nearly all below ground to take advantage of the natural warmth of the earth. In addition to sinking the whole structure a few feet into the ground, Bob insulated the exterior foundation walls and made a small vestibule at the east entrance as "a kind of air lock to keep the cool air from rushing through to the plants." A four-foot-deep planting bench against the south wall contains a combination of topsoil, manure, and potting soil, which also retains a certain amount of solar heat.

In the early days, when Lisa was at home, the raised beds contained all kinds of vegetables. The first winter they grew vegetables that tolerate cool nighttime temperatures, but they also experimented with several varieties of tomatoes. They found cherry tomatoes to be best, and their pick of leafy vegetables included Chinese white cabbage (bok choy) and Swiss chard. All the lettuces were a success. Their planting schedule was similar to the timetable followed by Eliot Coleman. Leafy crops started in August were ready for harvest by November.

In recent years Dodie has used the greenhouse as a winter home for ornamental plants by removing some of the planting medium to accommodate their pots. For a bit of extra color, she grows a ground cover of nasturtiums in the soil between them, explaining, "I take cuttings because it is much quicker than seeds and you get the colors you want. It's easy. All you do is cut off a few stems and remove the leaves. Lay the stems down on the soil, and you have new plants in no time."

Since the Freemans live near William Penn's "fine green Countrie Towne" of Philadelphia, it is not surprising that they have been involved for many years with the Philadelphia Flower Show. For the 1995 show, they did their bit as usual. "There are three days of the week when the plants come and go in the horticultural court," Dodie says. "Friday afternoon and Saturday morning, the plants come in for competitions and have to have certain paperwork. Each plant has to come to a 'passer,' who decides where it belongs and whether it is in good condition and so forth. We're the passers' aides. Then there's the 'stager,' who actually places the plant in the show."

Bob says the anticipation gets them through the winter. Until three years ago, preparation of their own exhibits occupied every waking moment from New Year's Day until the opening of the show in March. Like the solar greenhouse, their entries for the Miniature Settings Class were family affairs. Bob designed and built the displays, Lisa furnished the live plant material, and Dodie painted the walls, furniture, and decorative details of these exquisite scale-model garden settings.

When a friend of the Freemans' learned of my proposed visit, she said, "Be sure you ask to see their miniature rooms and gardens." So after a tour of the greenhouse, we repaired to Bob's workshop. What is it that is so fascinating about miniature scenes? Peering into an Alice in Wonderland world is part of the fun, but discovery is the chief source of delight: the discovery that the windows of a Victorian house the size of a cereal box are made of glass laboratory slides, that the fretwork of the porch was made with an ordinary paper punch, and that the intricate corner pieces of a minute screen door were cut from a paper doily. I was especially enthralled by the recreations of real places, such as a community garden in the heart of the inner city, with beds of minuscule vegetables and flowers, a trash can, and even microscopic graffiti painted on the tenement walls.

Another miniature scene depicted a gala evening event at the Philadelphia Art Museum. Bob described the actual setting: "The museum is up on a rocky sort of hill, looking down the parkway to City Hall. There is a lovely terrace, and once in a while they put up tents and tables and have a big benefit for the museum. We called this 'Toast to Philadelphia.' See the taillights of the cars going in and the headlights coming out?" Directly below the terrace, the red glow of paired taillights retreat in one direction, while bright white headlights advance from the other. On the miniature terrace the round tables are beautifully appointed with napery, candles, and flowers, and in the distance the Philadelphia skyline glitters with tiny lights.

Dodie planned to enter a small dried arrangement at the 1995 Philadelphia Flower Show, but the Freemans retired from miniature competition in 1992. Dodie's rationale was typical: "We thought it was time to get out, because you've got to make room . . . The last three years we got the blue ribbon and the silver trophy. We figured that Bob got a bowl, I got a bowl, and Lisa got a bowl. It's time to go. People would come up and say, 'Oh, I don't have a chance because you're in it.' That's not good. It's better to get out and go on to something else. We've had a lot of fun since, trying to help some of the newcomers."

Gary and Colleen Allen

Great Cranberry Island is one of the many small, fir-clad islands off the coast of Maine. Two and a half miles long, about half a mile wide, and shaped like the letter C, it lies just east of Mount Desert Island, a half-hour ferry ride from Northeast Harbor. Here, Gary and Colleen Allen have constructed a brand-new solar greenhouse, using Bob Freeman's plans.

As the crow flies, the Cranberry Isles are only thirty miles from Harborside, where Eliot Coleman and Barbara Damrosch tend their tunnel-covered cold frames, but getting from there to the Allens' by road and ferry takes over two hours. Dozens of byways run up and down the peninsulas of this much-indented coast. When you finally arrive at Northeast Harbor, after considerable backing and filling, there is still the boat ride to Great Cranberry Island.

On a summer day, getting there really is half the fun. From the water, the views of the other islands, the mainland, and the bold blue hills of Mount Desert Island are spectacular. Cadillac Mountain is the highest point. Rising abruptly from the flat plane of the sea, it appears much loftier than its modest 1,500 feet. Beneath a crystal-clear sky, the miles of visible shoreline are a study in royal blue and forest green.

During the summer months, a little passenger ferry plies the route from Northeast Harbor to the Cranberry Isles on a regular schedule, but off-season it runs only once a day. Nevertheless, hardy islanders like Gary and Colleen take the isolation and the long winters in their stride. Besides the sixteen-by-twenty-four-foot solar greenhouse, they have constructed a snug, handsome log home for themselves with a deep front porch, rough-hewn steps, and a wonderful handrail made from a gnarled apple bough. "We built this all ourselves," Gary told me with ill-concealed pride. Inside, the house is beautiful and full of light from generous windows that overlook a pond and the woods beyond.

Young, energetic, and optimistic, the Allens are now in the process of clearing more land and starting a small nursery to supply the island's summer population with annuals, perennials, and vegetables. They plan to grow all their own plants and to that end completed the greenhouse just in time for the vicious winter of 1993–1994. To their delight, the unheated structure proved effective and economical beyond their wildest fantasies.

Gary was exultant. "The great thing about these solar greenhouses is that they work. The damn things really work! When we were about half finished building ours, we talked to some commercial greenhouse people on the mainland, and they said, 'Naw, that won't work. That's a hippy green-house.'" What tickled the Allens was learning that their detractors were paying up to $500 a month for heat, while they spent nothing. "A plastic greenhouse is just so inefficient," Gary points out. "During the day it warms up, but you have to keep pumping heat into it all night long. And here we were starting our seedlings for free — for absolutely free! We have electricity in the greenhouse now, but we didn't put it in until spring, and the reason we needed it then was not for heat but because we were working such late hours transplanting and things."

Despite the long working days, the Allens' enjoyment of all that they do is palpable. In the summer, masses of bright annual flowers and ripening tomatoes outside the solar greenhouse bear witness to the success of their new venture. At the time of my visit, Colleen pointed out the benches where it all began. "This is where we started all the plants. We started them from seed, some in January, some later." January proved too early for the bego-nias, which had to be lugged back and forth between the greenhouse and the warm cabin. Colleen laughed and admitted, "The begonias were certainly intensive!"

However, considering the extreme weather, the Allens were very pleased with the performance of the greenhouse. Colleen said, "In January it got down to fifteen degrees below zero, but it was forty-seven degrees in here. It is really wonderful, when you think that we did not use any supplementary heat at all." They do, however, have night curtains, which she says are critical. Nighttime heat loss is a problem with all passive solar structures. The word "passive" means that no auxiliary energy source is employed; the system is totally dependent on the sun.

During the planning stages, the Allens were disappointed to discover that the literature on solar greenhouses offered no easy solutions to radia-tional cooling. Gary failed to find "any really well-thought-out solar blan-kets for nighttime use." Bob Freeman complained of the same problem and devised bifold panels of stiff insulation board. Gary settled for a lightweight, flexible insulation material. It is thin enough to store in a gigantic roll suspended from the ceiling.

"This stuff is made for thermal protection," he says. "It's basically foil on two sides over bubble-wrap, and it really has a huge resistance to heat traveling through it." Colleen explains its conventional building uses: "You put it in your attic to discourage heat loss, and a lot of people wrap their hot water heater and pipes in it. That's what it's for. And it works for us, but we still have some kinks to work out before the real cold weather sets in again. The biggest one is that I can't roll it up and down by myself. I'm not quite tall enough or strong enough. We really need some kind of pulley system. For now, it's Gary's baby."

Clumsy as the great sheet of silver-colored material may be, it does a remarkable job. It keeps the stored heat in and sharply reduces radiational cooling. The Allens did exhaustive research into materials and concluded that this works well compared to other solar blankets. Gary, whose chore it is to put the greenhouse to bed, marvels at the difference in temperature. "When we installed this blanket, we experienced a twelve-degree increase in the nighttime temperature. Before, it was getting down into the low to mid-thirties in here. When we added this, it jumped up into the mid-forties and above. You do get some heat loss through the glazed portion of the building, but this really helped."

From the gable end, the Allens' greenhouse looks almost like a small shingled saltbox. The roof slopes at a normal angle to the north and at a long steep angle to the south. It is obvious that Gary made a number of departures from Bob's design, and he explained his reasons. "For one thing, the angle of his roof, which is geared to the latitude in Pennsylvania, is actually flatter than ours. The farther north you go, the steeper the angle gets. When you get far enough north — up toward the Arctic Circle — you could actually build one of these greenhouses with a vertical roof, because the angle of the sun would be almost horizontal."

Bob's A-frame is partially underground, with a poured concrete and cement-block foundation. Because the expense of importing such heavy materials from the mainland would have been prohibitive, the Allens' version is freestanding. It rests on six-by-six-inch wooden sills, cleverly anchored to the site with six-by-six posts sunk into the ground.

To compensate for the exposed aboveground walls, the Allens added rigid foam insulation two inches thick on the outside. First they dug a trench all around the building. Installing the four-by-eight-foot panels proved tricky. The seams and corners had to fit perfectly, and the backfilling had to be done by hand. "We did it carefully with shovels, not machinery, so as not to break the panels," Gary explains. Long-lasting and rot-resistant, the insulation now extends down four feet on all sides, deep enough to prevent the earth floor inside from freezing. The floor itself provides a modicum of extra heat and, like the Freemans', is topped off with a foot of crushed rock.

While the Allens didn't build a replica of Bob's A-frame, they did follow gratefully in his footsteps. "He took wonderful notes, from step one through finish," says Colleen, "and he shared everything with us. He put some permanent beds in his greenhouse. We copied him and put in a little one here, but we haven't used it yet. That's another exciting thing we're going to do this winter — grow things right in the earth in here."

As I write, Colleen must already be sowing seeds and dreaming of the new season.

Gluttons for Punishment

You will understand this chapter better if I let Avery Larned fill you in on a lifestyle that is no longer familiar to everyone. "Farmers started doing maple sugaring," she explains, "because winter is the dead season for them. It's one of the only things you can do with the land at that time of year. Plus, it is a big cash crop. It's a way to buy a new tractor and new equipment. You spend six weeks making maple syrup. You sell it for a lot of money. All of a sudden you have two thousand dollars right there in your hand. Then you can go out and buy new equipment, and you're right at the beginning of the farming season. Traditionally, sugaring is a very common thing for farmers to do."

Figuring that her mother, Joan Larned, had an orchard and was therefore a farmer, Avery decided that sugaring would be a good thing for them to do in the winter. "Farmers," says Joan, "are gluttons for punishment. They love to go out and chop wood and haul sap."

At the moment Avery is in the Smith College School for Social Work master's program, but she moonlights for Outward Bound and lives in Maine, "sort of." Recently she has been working as an intern at an adolescent counseling center. But wherever she is and whatever else she is doing, she always comes home to Connecticut for the maple sugaring season.

Joan and Avery Larned

Since 1985, when Joan planted the orchard, winters have seemed too short to her. "My summers and falls are so busy that they run right into springs," she says. As a fruit grower with three hundred apple trees and three hundred peach trees to tend, she barely finishes the autumn cleanup before it's time to start spring pruning — February for the apples, later for the peaches.

Like any farmer, she has to juggle these chores according to temperature and weather. January 1995 was unseasonably warm, and she got a headstart on the pruning. The maple sugaring season begins about a month later. The sugarbush — a group or grove of sugar maples (*Acer saccharum*) — is a joint effort with Avery.

Avery became excited about the whole sugaring process when she was working in Vermont. "After I graduated from college in the mid-eighties," she explains, "I got this great job at a maple research center affiliated with the University of Vermont. I was involved scientifically with maple trees, but we also learned to make maple syrup." Every year she taps five hundred of the one thousand or more maples on her mother's property and processes the sap into maple syrup. "I'm her assistant," says Joan. "We started the sugaring business at the same time that I put in the orchard."

The orchard and a half-acre blueberry patch are fairly recent developments. In 1984, after a course in orcharding at Cornell University, Joan signed up for the integrated pest management program offered by the University of Connecticut Department of Plant Science. She loved it, and describes it as "a wonderful program designed to help orchardists use fewer chemicals in managing their trees." The following year, to the astonishment of friends, she quit her New York City life to grow fruit trees in Connecticut.

Why would a sixty-year-old woman with a perfectly good job in Manhattan — a job that she liked — suddenly leave the city to start a fruit farm? Joan never needed to ask herself that question. The answer lay in the sixty-eight acres she had just inherited from her mother. A family tradition of land conservation and a sturdy belief in the work ethic were reason enough. "I hate to see land idle," she says. Equally, she would have hated to see the patchwork of fields and wooded hills she has loved since childhood subdivided into building lots.

Millstone Farm has been in Joan's family for three generations. Her maternal grandparents bought the eighteenth-century farmhouse, barn, and four hundred acres of rolling meadows. At that time the property stretched eastward to the shore of Lake Waramaug. To my mind, Waramaug is one of the loveliest lakes in a state well endowed with attractive bodies of water. Like the tarns and meres of England's Lake District, it is completely enveloped by folds of the surrounding hills. Thanks to the generosity of Joan's mother and two aunts, part of this beauty has been preserved from development as Lake Waramaug State Park.

The remaining acres were handed down to Joan. These lie west of the lake and are separated from it by woodland and the local country club. Joan's road is narrow, with fields on either side enclosed by old stone walls. The fields are now planted with fruit trees. Along the road and close to the stone walls stand venerable sugar maples. These "wolf trees," so called because their broad canopies devour space and inhibit the development of smaller trees, are reminders of a bygone era. Protected by the walls, they escaped the scythe and later the mowing machine.

Joan calls the majestic survivors "bucket trees," because at sugaring time they are tapped and fitted with covered buckets to collect the sap. Sap from the smaller maples flows via a network of flexible plastic tubing directly into a storage tank. In keeping with her notion that land should be used, she welcomed Avery's sugaring operation. "It's fun," she says. "And I love it . . . when it's over."

Avery echoed her mother's sentiments when a local newspaper reporter interviewed her in 1992: "You go into this with the idea that you do it because you love it . . . Well, by the end of the season I hate it, but a week after it's over, I can't wait for next year!"

The maintenance work begins in January — cleaning the sap lines, fixing the evaporator, and hauling wood. Gathering, sawing, and splitting logs are ongoing winter tasks. A neighbor with a passion for cutting down trees helps out, but it falls to Avery to go into the woods with tractor and chains to drag out the logs. She and Joan cut anything under four inches with a gas-powered chain saw, and they share a powerful new hydraulic log splitter with several of their neighbors.

Avery built the Larneds' sugarhouse, which looks like a small red barn surmounted by an oversize cupola. The sides of the cupola are open to the elements to vent steam generated by the Grimm evaporator below. Sap is piped into a holding tank behind the sugarhouse. From the tank it flows into stainless steel pans, where it is boiled down into syrup. The heat is provided by a cast-iron firebox underneath the pans, and a mixture of hard and soft wood is fed through doors at one end. The firebox consumes six or seven cords of wood each season in the sugarmaking process.

As I discovered in the course of talking to Joan, maple sugaring is not for sissies. The next time you pour a curling amber stream over warm pancakes, think about this. If you were to make a pint of this delicious concoction in your kitchen, you would need five gallons of raw sap. The vat of sap has to be brought to a rolling boil and boiled continually for five hours. The resulting steam would probably denude your walls of paper, and the gas or electricity bill would make a large hole in your pocketbook. Alternatively, you could huddle in your woolies outdoors in the garden, presiding over a jerrybuilt evaporator made from a metal trashcan.

For even a small-scale commercial operation, it takes between thirty and forty gallons of sap to make one gallon of syrup. At Millstone Farm, the lifeblood of five hundred sugar maples, flowing at a variable rate over a period of approximately four to five weeks, yields enough sap to make about one hundred gallons of syrup.

Collecting, boiling, and condensing the sap are daily chores that cannot be postponed or deferred. Once the sap has been collected, it goes rancid unless it is processed quickly. And processing means manning the wood fire under the evaporator until the sap has been reduced to syrup. Avery says that during peak flow, her days begin before 7 A.M. and seldom end until after midnight.

The whimsical weather of southern New England makes sugaring a particular challenge. Sap starts to flow when the days begin to lengthen and daytime temperatures rise above freezing. Daytime highs in the forties and nights below freezing are ideal. But ideal conditions rarely last.

In Connecticut, the sap usually starts flowing the last week in February, and the season ends with the appearance on the tree of the first buds. However, the rush of sap can start anytime there is an extended warm spell. Slowed by the sudden return of cold temperatures, it may resume for a while, then be cut short by the premature arrival of spring.

Joan's kitchen windows look out on the sugarbush, which borders a huge open field. The field slopes downhill to the north, and in the absence of snow cover the winter grasses are a uniform tan against the blue Litchfield hills in the distance. At the bottom of the incline, a single row of impressive, well-spaced maples stands sentinel along the stone wall. I was told that these trees are called the Hicks run, after favorite neighbors.

On the eastern boundary of the field, the trees merge into woodland. The maples here are young and gregarious, growing cheek by jowl with other species. Farther into the woods, the ground drops sharply. A little ravine runs parallel to the edge of the field, and the main pipeline of the sap-collecting operation, a long bright blue hose an inch in diameter, descends the hill, following the course of the ravine. It terminates in a five-hundred-gallon storage tank. Maples at the edge of the field are connected by umbilical cords of thin plastic tubing to the main line, and the sap is borne downhill by the pull of gravity. On the opposite side of the ravine, the web of secondary tubing stretches deep into the woods.

Avery acknowledges invaluable help in laying out the system from her mentor in Vermont. "When Mom and I started talking about a sugaring operation here," she says, "the guy who taught me came down to Connecticut and walked the woods with us. We talked about the slope of the hill and set up an imaginary tubing system, which we actually duplicated the following year."

When the weather is right and the sap is flowing, the sugarhouse becomes a lively, entertaining place. Groups of schoolchildren, as colorful as Easter eggs in their multicolored parkas, caps, and scarves, come to observe the sugaring process and hang around to play in the soft, wet snow that often ushers in the season. Joan's grandchildren are frequent visitors and enliven the proceedings.

Her house on the family property is a refurbished barn, its fine old post-and-beam pattern exposed against the white plaster walls. Her front windows overlook the garden that her grandmother made, which Joan has restored. Although it is not the same as when her mother and aunts played on the grass paths as children, it has the feel of the old garden. A Yankee interpretation of an enclosed English garden, it has embracing walls made with the same gray fieldstones the local farmers used to fashion their boundary fences. Within the ample square enclosure, broad paths divide the space into quadrants. There are still perennial borders along the paths, and in season an abundance of old-fashioned flowers — shrub roses, blue and white campanulas, and pink peonies from the original garden. Two large crab-apple trees frame a bench at the end of the main axial path. Beyond, the orchard marches across the fields.

Recently Joan sold some of her fruit trees. "I'm not moving out of this phase of my life," she explains, "but you have to move on. Change is good. That's the way life is." Resilient and down-to-earth, she has absorbed both the lessons and the hard knocks of a varied and interesting life. Even as a girl, she displayed an independent spirit that made her spurn a comfortable and familiar berth in an Eastern women's college. Brought up on Staten Island, New York, she chose instead the University of Wisconsin and adventure. She had an idea that she wanted to be a landscape architect. When she met with nothing but opposition — women were not encouraged to compete with men in those days — she did the next best thing. She went into occupational therapy, because it involved some study of the arts.

The return from World War II of "the boy next door" put paid to her career in that field. She had been thirteen when Jack Larned went away. When he came back, wearing "a beautiful uniform," she was nineteen and susceptible. They were married at the end of her sophomore year and soon had four children and a hectic suburban life.

Jack was an advertising man in New York, but he had an idea. In 1969 many African countries had recently achieved independence, and Jack saw there a crying need for a business program that would teach basic management skills. He jumped in, founding the nonprofit International Management Development Institute and taking his family with him. Joan recalls those years with pleasure: "We were an itinerant group and lived in eleven different African countries. It was very exciting, and I loved it. I made arrangements for everyone, because we had people from all over Africa and we always had to house them at facilities that had classroom space. I did everything from changing light bulbs to planning meals."

Tragedy ended the African adventure. On a visit home in 1973, Jack was killed in an automobile accident. Avery, their youngest child, was eleven at the time. A year later, Joan went back to school. She completed first her bachelor's degree and then a master's in developmental psychology, receiving her diploma the day before her daughter Debby's marriage. "Thinking back, I don't know how Avery grew up," she says ruefully. But the family flourished, and Joan went to work as a career counselor. Then the farm suddenly became hers.

Once quoted by an interviewer as saying, "I can't see any relationships between all the things I've done," Joan now rejects this view. Instead, she sees the disparate threads of her life drawing together here at Millstone Farm — family, friends, former students; what she has learned; what she has done; what she has taught. As she puts it, "When I worked in career counseling, we used to say to our students, 'Nothing you do is for naught.' It's true."

Making It Through the Winter

Our basement is not the sort of place where you would want to spend a lot of time, especially in the winter. When the house was built in the early nineteenth century, there wasn't much call for headroom. With no heating system or plumbing to accommodate, houses sat tightly wedded to the earth. They had fieldstone foundations and cellars with dirt floors, if they had cellars at all. While our basement is a cut above that, it isn't inviting. It has a cement floor, an old foundation where snakes are known to hibernate. (In the spring, they emerge and coil themselves around the transformer for warmth.) The areaway windows don't let in much light, and the temperature can rarely be coaxed above sixty degrees.

Nevertheless, I spend a few afternoons down there every winter making lath shades to protect plants from the direct sunlight. It is a simple winter project that pays enormous dividends when the transplanting season arrives. The A-frame shades are meant to conserve moisture in the plants' foliage and root zone while admitting light and air. My husband designed them, and I build them, using one-by-two-inch furring strips for the side pieces and plaster lath for the slats.

The most economical size is a two-foot-square model. Lath comes by the bundle in four-foot lengths, and precut furring strips eight feet long are the easiest size to handle. Each lath yields two slats and each furring strip four side pieces. Two identical frames are joined at the top to make the A-frame. The shades are very useful, so useful that people often borrow them and seldom return them.

Winter craft projects for or from the garden can be as crude as my A-frame shades or as exquisite as the finest cabinetwork. In this chapter you will meet people who have raised their garden-related crafts to high levels of beauty and utility. Not every gardener has the dexterity or desire to master these skills, but if you have never thought of learning basketry or carpentry, spinning or weaving, why not give one of them a try?

Hugh and Hope Davis

When November arrives, darkness falls early, and Hugh Davis brings his antique shave horse indoors. His winter project is making parts for Marsh Wobble Gate Fences. Hewn from white cedar with an old-fashioned draw-knife, these charming, rustic structures look like sections of a miniature split rail fence, with the addition of two diagonal braces. I fell in love with them at Betsy Williams's shop in Andover, Massachusetts. "In that case," said Betsy, "you should meet Hope and Hugh Davis. They would be perfect in your winter book. She's a wonderful gardener, and he can make anything." My subsequent trip to the Farmstead in Leverett, Massachusetts, proved her right.

Reversing the trend toward separation of work and pleasure, home and office, his and hers, the Davises have woven their lives and livelihood together. The Farmstead is home, garden, nursery, and cottage industry rolled into one. Hope raises herbs and perennials for the local farmers' market; Hugh creates garden accessories from wood and helps with the nursery. In the winter she tends her seedlings under lights in an upstairs bedroom, and he puts the shave horse on the hearth of their huge keeping room fireplace and turns out gates.

A recent order from Longwood Gardens has kept Hugh busy producing the gates as fast as he can. Hope found the prototype at Great Dixter, the garden of the eminent British horticulturist and writer Christopher Lloyd. "We were there in early April," she recalls, "and it was wet. They had one placed across a muddy path to discourage visitors from going that way. I knew right away that Hugh could probably make them. So we bought one. I think I remember having it on my lap in the plane. We've found lots of new uses for them. They seem to hold plants up very nicely, and I like to use them to delineate a rectangular garden area. Having two at right angles at the four corners of the garden gives you a sense of definition."

Hugh loves his shave horse, which is one of the most primitive but effective of antique tools. "It's the neatest thing — it's so simple and clever and functional," he says. It looks a bit like a cobbler's bench. He sits at one end and draws the knife toward him. In addition to the gates, he makes handsome doormats from oak, and someday he plans to grow broom corn and add handmade brooms to his repertoire. A type of corn developed specially for broom-making used to be a major cash crop here in the Connecticut River Valley, and he intends to revive this local tradition.

Hugh's extraordinary craftsmanship is responsible for the beauty and authenticity of the Davises' magnificent eighteenth-century saltbox. Once a dilapidated, chimneyless shell held together only by its sound old beams, the house was rescued and restored by Hugh. He and Hope, with the help of his two brothers, took the building down beam by beam, floorboard by floorboard, and transported it to its present situation on a rise overlooking a pond, fields, and woodland.

In the 1960s, the Davises didn't know too much about old houses, except that they liked them. A native of New Jersey, Hope had loved New England houses since her first visit to Massachusetts as a teenager. "I happened to come up here one summer when I was about fifteen, and I loved everything about the place. I thought, 'This is where I want to live. This is home,'" she says. Hugh grew up nearby and felt an affinity for the local architecture, but acquisition of their handyman's paradise triggered a serious quest for information about period fireplace and chimney construction.

Hope traveled to the Society for the Preservation of New England Antiquities, in Boston, to do research, while Hugh made occasional visits to Washington, D.C., to consult WPA drawings of old buildings. Then, just as they were beginning the work of reconstruction, a young man who knew a lot about old houses turned up. He said he would like to advise the Davises as they went along, and they were happy to accept his offer.

First he told them that they would have to have quarter-cut clapboards for the siding. "Quarter cut" is a special way of sawing the logs so that all the grain is parallel. Hugh duly wrote to every county extension agent in northern Vermont and finally located a mill that produced quarter-cut clapboards.

Next the young man asked the Davises what kind of nails they planned to use. The upshot was that Hugh made all the rosehead nails for the house. "He told us to go to the nail company and buy the rods. You heat a bit of rod on a little hearth, whack it to a point, drop it down, and whack it three times to make the head," Hugh explains. When I asked him how he came by his innumerable skills, he shrugged and said, "I was raised on a farm here in Massachusetts, and you sort of learn to do things."

One of the things he learned to do was operate a backhoe. At one time his nephew, now a veterinarian, had an excavation business, and whenever he didn't need his backhoe, he would leave it at the Farmstead. "We did everything with that machine," Hugh remembers wistfully. They laid the huge slabs of stone for the front walk and the massive front doorsteps. Hugh found the stones for the walk in Vernon, Connecticut, where an old church had burned down. He bought them for a song. The granite blocks for the front doorsteps he swapped for a bottle of scotch. When the house was finished, he found a barn for $300 — a bargain he couldn't resist. He and the couple's two sons took the pickup truck to the site, dismantled the barn, and hauled it home. With winter approaching, the sensible thing to do was to stack the lumber and wait for spring. They had, of course, taken the precaution of numbering each piece with a wax pencil, but by spring the wax had worn off, and they were confronted with "a huge Tinker Toy — and no directions." However, they succeeded in piecing it together like a puzzle. Today, both barn and house look as if they have been standing there for the past two hundred years.

The splendid old saltbox faces north. According to Hope, it would have been sited the other way around originally, but she wanted a southern exposure for the keeping room — the long room at the back that now serves as kitchen, dining room, and living room. "I wanted the keeping room to face south for the winter sun," she explained. "And it works out well. On sunny days the room is flooded with light. In the summer we don't get that much light, because the angle of the sun is higher, but it doesn't matter because we're outdoors anyway."

Inside, the rooms are large, beautifully proportioned, and furnished sparingly with period pieces. Even what is new looks old. In the keeping room, there are Shaker-style cupboards made by the Davises' cabinetmaker son. Small-paned casement windows offer a lovely view of the garden. In summer the deep overhang of the eaves shades the windows, which are flung wide, allowing the interior and exterior space to flow together. Pale pink 'Fairy' roses and tall spires of delphinium rise from white clouds of feverfew and strain upward toward the open windows.

At first Hope considered making an eighteenth-century garden. "Having this old house, I wanted herbs and some of the old-fashioned flowers. I was thinking in terms of making the whole thing authentic, a museum kind of thing," she says. "But as I got into it, I realized, 'My God, I love everything! I want to grow everything!' So I scrapped the whole idea of complete authenticity. We've got new and old, but I did want to grow things that have the *feeling* of an old garden, although they might be new cultivars."

There is nothing like owning a house and a piece of ground to quicken the gardening instinct. Hope had always loved flowers but lacked the confidence to throw herself into gardening. It wasn't until she was presented with an old house on a raw new piece of land that she began to lose her inhibitions. "I discovered that this was something I loved to do and that it didn't take fine hand-eye coordination. I had tried to learn to sew and knit, but I never could do any of that. Gardening didn't seem to take that kind of precise handwork. I could prick out seedlings and they lived. Gardening kind of came naturally."

First, however, she learned more about historic landscapes. Ann Leighton's books on period gardens were her primary source of information. Leighton wrote three books: one on seventeenth-century gardens, another on eighteenth-, and, just before her death, one on nineteenth-century gardens. By the time Hope read the early books, she realized that there would have been no foundation planting around the house. "We didn't have a beautiful old stone foundation — we had a new one," she notes, "so I had to cover it a little and do some compromising. I used ivy in front and a couple of mountain laurels, which they never would have had. Actually, very little was planted around old houses." Authentic or not, the flowerbed beneath the casement windows at the back of the house has the look and charm of an eighteenth-century cottage garden.

A book about historic gardens by Rudy Favretti gave Hope the incentive to take his classes at the University of Connecticut, and in due course she received her master's degree in historic landscapes. While she learned a great deal from the program, she decided that she really did not want to be a scholar — "at least not in the summer. I was writing my thesis, and the library was air-conditioned. It was freezing cold. And here I was inside, when I wanted to be out in the garden. I like mucking around in the soil, and I *love* weeding. I can happily go out at eight o'clock in the morning and not come in until five."

The nursery evolved out of Hope's love of growing plants and her reluctance to throw things away. "I kept having all these extra plants, so I started taking a few to the farmers' market we have here in town. In the end, I was actually growing things for the market and going every week. It was fun. I found that I could grow certain things, and people would come back the next year and say, 'Hope, that plant I bought from you last year lived! It grew!' They would be so pleased, and that's good. I was helping to create new gardeners by having these foolproof things."

Propagation is Hope's department, but now that Hugh has retired from his teaching job at the University of Massachusetts, he does all the digging, dividing, and potting. He also makes the wooden frames that support Hope's raised stock beds. These edgings are both decorative and necessary to lift the plants above the high water table. I also admired the racks, like tiered picnic tables, that he constructed to display potted plants in the sales area. One of his projects this winter is to extend the intricate double picket fence that encloses part of the garden. He copied the design from a similar fence he saw outside the tourist office in Tewkesbury, England.

Hugh claims that he doesn't have much sense of design, but everything he makes is as handsome as it is functional. In the early eighties, he built a pit greenhouse for the winter storage of tender plants. Later he added an attractive potting shed. Hope doesn't think of herself as a designer either, but she has made those vital connections that hold the garden together — connections between house and outbuildings, stone walls, paths, and flowerbeds. The arrangement of the separate parts makes sense and fits into the semiwild surrounding landscape. For two people to create so much that is essential and beautiful — with an absolute minimum of outside help — is an astonishing achievement.

Mary and Dick Kordes

Winter in northern Michigan usually starts in mid-October, with a heavy snowfall while the autumn leaves are still on the trees. "The red or yellow trees brushed with a whipped-cream snow are a pretty sight," writes Mary Kordes. "As the snow weighs down the aging leaves, they fall to the ground, sprinkling the new white snowcover with splashes of color, all yellow or all red, under their respective trees. But this snow is just a teaser — a taste of what's to come. Our real winter begins about the third week of November. By that time, it's cold enough for squalls to develop over Lake Superior and snow to start piling up on the ground."

Everyone who lives on the Keweenaw Peninsula is attuned to the weather. In that sparsely populated region, people think ahead when a winter storm is forecast and rush to the store to stock up on groceries. Until their retirement, Mary and Dick Kordes owned a grocery store and used to find the sudden influx of customers exhilarating.

"In the old days of the Ahmeek Mining Company, root vegetables were the mainstay of the kitchen, and even in our day, cabbages, rutabagas, and potatoes were our biggest sellers in the winter," Mary says. During the nineteenth century, the copper-rich peninsula attracted miners from Cornwall, England, and Cornish pasties, made of vegetables and meat encased in pastry, are still popular cold-weather fare.

Mary and Dick bought their grocery store in the village of Ahmeek twenty years ago and ran it for sixteen years. Dick was the butcher for most of that time, and they both worked long days. But they loved the life, the people, and most of all the countryside around them. Every spare moment they would spend exploring the beaches, tramping in the woods, and sifting through the piles of "poor rock" — basalt discarded from mining operations — looking for bits of copper. "One of our favorite family outings when our children were young was climbing around on the poor-rock piles," Mary continues. "There were many whoops of delight when we found even tiny pieces with the telltale verdigris color and sharp points formed by molten copper seeping into cracks in the existing lava flows."

During the grocery store years, a small flower garden was all that Mary could manage, but her lifetime love of gardening blossomed indoors. Every windowsill in their apartment above the store was filled with plants. The overflow found its way down to the store windows, giving pleasure to the customers as well.

Mary remembers, "Our winter evenings were busy even in those years.

We polished agates and other stones that we found during stolen summer hours on the beach. Dick and I began weaving baskets, and I made wreaths of pine cones, dried weeds, seedpods, and mosses I had gathered in the fall. Dick did some woodcarving, and I did a bit of weaving and dyed yarns with plant materials, because I loved the muted hues and the process fascinated me."

For the fun of it one winter, they took Ground School flight-training classes and passed their FAA written exams — as Mary puts it, "with flying colors." They even started the actual flight training and found it "a great experience." But flying was too expensive as a hobby. Instead, they both took the Master Gardener course offered by Michigan State University through the extension service, feeling that the forty-mile round trip was worth it. But the winter that bore the richest fruit was the one Dick spent drafting and fine-tuning the plan for their retirement home.

They had owned the land for years. On a long-ago Sunday, they had ridden their bicycles out into the country. Four miles north of Ahmeek, they fell in love with a tree-crowned knoll. There were maples, some tall spruce, and a small grove of birches. First they leased the forty-seven-acre parcel from the mining company that still owned the property, but a few years later they were able to buy it outright. "That's when our dream of scooping out a pond in the tangle of wetland in front of our knoll became a reality," Mary says.

In 1990 they began building the house. Dick wanted the basement walls to be extra high to give him headroom for a workshop, so they hired a mason to do the foundations. They also called in help to raise the outer wall frames. The rest Dick did himself, with Mary as gofer. On November 14, 1991, two days before the snows began in earnest, they moved in.

Most winter days now, Dick works in the woods surrounding their home. He dons felt-lined boots and bundles himself into a one-piece Day-Glo orange snowsuit with a wool cap pulled firmly down over his ears. Because the ground is covered with three or four feet of snow, snowshoes are an essential part of his equipment. Strapped into the webbed snowshoes, he sets off into the woods with his long aluminum ladder and pruning saw. He cuts dead wood and removes small, weedy trees that interfere with the growth habit of the larger specimens. He clears walking trails and continues to push back the forest to accommodate more gardens.

When it is impossibly cold and the wind-chill factor is too discouraging, he spends the days in his basement workshop, fashioning beautiful things for their beloved house and garden. For the house, there are elegant baskets, boxes, turned finials, and brackets to hold up the curtain rods. For the garden, he has built a special propagation frame.

Mary found a drawing of the frame in one of the bulletins of the North American Rock Garden Society. The night he finished it, they went out and sited it by the stars to make sure it was aligned due north. Mary reports that they have rooted many cuttings in the new frame, and Dick is constantly on the lookout for witches' brooms, abnormal, bushlike growths sometimes found on spruces and other woody plants, which can give rise to dwarf specimens. "He'd like to try starting dwarf trees from them," Mary says, "but we haven't found information on the proper time to make the cuttings yet."

In 1992, Dick built Mary a small unheated greenhouse from wood they harvested on the property. Although it is too cold to use the greenhouse before March, it gives them a head start on the growing season. They order their seeds in January and start them under fluorescent lights in the basement. By April, Dick's tomato, pepper, cabbage, celery, and onion plants are ready to be moved out to the greenhouse during the day. This makes room under the lights for Mary to germinate the pots of primrose seeds and other hardy perennials that she has left outside all winter. These seeds need the cold and moisture to break their dormancy.

It was primroses that brought Mary into my life. Several years ago, I wrote an article about primulas. As the daughter of an expatriate Briton, I had always found the common English primrose (*Primula vulgaris*) to have particular significance. It was my mother's favorite flower and the inspiration for my woodland garden. From that sentimental starting point, I began growing other species of primulas. Those that do best in my zone 6 Connecticut garden are from the cool, damp meadows of Europe or those islands of Japan that have a climate similar to mine.

To make a long story short, Mary read the primrose article and became hooked. She has long since surpassed me in the number of species that flourish in her garden, but I have the infinite satisfaction of having pointed her in this direction. With typical generosity, she wrote to me about the article: "I feel compelled to tell you I consider you the very special person who opened my life to the world of primulas. My collection is still growing, but they have given me so much color and joy. My first primrose seedlings were from a package of mixed *Primula* 'Pacific Giants'. I also have a nice patch of *P. denticulata*, a pale lavender color. There are a few *P. japonica*, magenta color, and some 'Postford White'; a *P. veris* plant, and some pale yellow *P. elatior*. My one plant of *P. florindae* bloomed for the first time last summer. Most of my plants are seed-grown, and I've never seen any of the species before, except in photos in books. I'm nearly prying some of the blossoms open, I'm so anxious to see them!"

And so our correspondence began. Mary writes more and better letters, but I call and write when I can. She has sent me northern snow bedstraw (*Galium boreale*), pink and white mallows (*Malva moschata*), and burgundy bladder campion (*Silene vulgaris*) for my garden, and I have added *Primula abschasica* to her collection. I tell her about the fat mockingbird that spends the winter denuding our winterberry; she describes their flock of tame chickadees and the wonderful waterfowl that frequent their pond. I complain of white-tailed deer; she regales me with tales of the black bear that sat on Dick's kohlrabi.

In Connecticut, the lilacs bloom in May; on the Keweenaw Peninsula, they bloom a month later. On June 11, 1994, Mary wrote, "It's Lilac Time in the Copper Country. There are lilacs everywhere. Ancient plants still grow and blossom where the tiny log homes of early miners once stood, and young escapee lilacs dot the landscape."

In the same letter she told me about the drive she and Dick had taken with her elderly mother and stepfather. "They were as delighted as children — Dick and I were, too. We made a list of the wildflowers we saw in bloom so that Mom can sit and read it and relive the day." There were flowering trees and wild shrubs: pincherry trees and chokecherry bushes, thorn apples and wild mountain ash. "Marsh marigolds, wood anemones, and forget-me-nots made big pools and swaths of color. And the wild roses, oxeye daisies, orange hawkweed, and wild lupines were beginning to bloom. I would so love to have had you with us, Sydney! It's a special time of year, but it seems there is always something to look for on the Keweenaw, no matter what the time of year."

When the world is too much with me, I think about that countryside and the rock-strewn lakeshore. Forced upward by the weight of an ancient glacier, the tilting slabs of stone are brick red. Lake Superior, as blue and vast as an ocean, laps at their feet. Above the rocks, the hilly terrain is clothed with birch, spruce, fir, white pine, maple, and oak.

Underlying this sylvan world, a warren of manmade tunnels penetrates deep into the bedrock. This is Copper Country. Only the White Pine Copper Mine, at the southernmost end of the peninsula, is still in operation and making a profit, but in the early 1840s the whole area seethed with activity. The newspaper serving Houghton, Keweenaw, Baraga, and Ontonagon counties is still called the *Daily Mining Gazette,* and in June 1994 the House of Representatives approved a substantial grant for a national historic park devoted to preserving the Copper Country's rich mining history.

Mary's forebears came to this remote tip of Michigan from Cornwall in 1867. It took her great-great-grandfather two years down in the mines to work off his passage and save enough to send for his wife and children. None of his sons chose to go underground. Instead, three became lighthouse keepers along the shores of the peninsula. Another became the head book-keeper for two mining companies.

Today, Mary's mother and stepfather live in the old Ahmeek Mining Company pay-office building. Mary wrote, "Mom and Dad bought it nearly thirty years ago, a solid brick and local sandstone structure that once housed the bookkeeping and payroll offices. When Great-Great-Grandpa could no longer go down in the mines, he worked there as a janitor. Mom's great-uncle was head bookkeeper there. And her father, my grandfather, was also a bookkeeper in that building. So it has a lot of sentimental value."

Early in their married life, Mary and Dick lived near their hometown of Milwaukee, where he worked as a machinist, but their hearts belonged to the Keweenaw Peninsula. For her, it had always been a special place. It was part of her heritage. "I had been coming here since childhood for vacations with my parents," she explains. "Then Dick and I came on our honeymoon, and he too fell in love with the area. In reality, it's very rugged: rugged winters, rugged terrain, rugged coastline, and vicious blackflies for the six weeks of early summer. But it's a beautiful place. And there is so much here to enjoy."

Rita Buchanan

Rita Buchanan describes herself as a "do-stuff-with-real-things sort of person," and the two things she has done for almost as long as she can remember are growing plants and making cloth. On a recent winter morning, with snow still covering the ground, we sat in her lean-to greenhouse surrounded by a jungle of plants and baskets containing homespun yarns in gorgeous natural colors.

Glancing around, I realized that Rita had either raised or made everything in the room. She grew most of the plants from seed, cuttings, or bulbs, knitted the sweater she was wearing from yarn spun right there in the greenhouse, and dyed the yarn with plants from her summer garden.

For her, the calendar year has a rhythm of its own: spring for sowing, summer for growing, fall for harvesting, and winter for spinning, weaving, and knitting. "On the one hand, I've always been involved with growing and studying plants. And the textile part of it, that's just something I've done evenings and weekends — well, forever," she says. "I think of growing plants as something to do outdoors when it's light and the weather is nice. Making textiles is something to do indoors when it's cold and dark outside."

Plants and the out-of-doors are my bailiwick, and I have enjoyed watching the development of Rita's garden. "From every window now, I can see something that I have done," she says with satisfaction. "Two years ago at this time, there was nothing but the sea of mud left over from the pond construction. I just didn't have a clue what we were getting into or if we'd ever be able to do it. But we've made a lot of progress since then, and finally it all seems possible."

A length of level lawn bordered by still youthful trees and shrubs unfolds toward the pond. A proposed bench on the opposite shore will one day provide a place to rest the viewer's eye and the gardener's body. A beautiful little curved bridge spans the stream as it leaves the pond and leads to the site of the bench. Another handsome footbridge crosses the creek that feeds the pond. A path on the other side disappears into a woodland dark with hemlocks. Rita's husband, Steve, built the bridges and is responsible for clearing trails all through the Buchanans' wooded acres, but she is the gardener here.

The spring and summer phases of Rita's year are familiar to me. I understand and can appreciate sowing, growing, and garden-making. The autumn rite of brewing dyes from home-grown woad, weld, and madder is another story. As for winters devoted to spinning wool into yarn and making cloth by hand, these activities are so far beyond my ken that they seem almost magical. To Rita, they are second nature. She has, tucked away in tissue paper, scraps of fine woolen material woven by her father's grandmother and great-grandmother. The yarn was spun at home from wool that came from the family sheep.

"I remember these kinds of pieces of cloth being in the house from the time I was a little kid," she explains, "so I had an early awareness that people make cloth. I grew up in a family that was old-fashioned and tied to the old ways, so that I took some things for granted. Historically, and even around the world today, most people do make cloth. It's only been in the last generation that we've come to think of cloth as something you buy."

As the youngest of five children, Rita grew up with the understanding that you make everything you use. Her parents came from a strong farming tradition and chose to preserve the lifestyle that they knew best and believed in. It was built on hard work, making, and making do. Self-sufficiency, self-respect, and independence were the rewards. Her father got up every morning and milked the cows before going to his job as an engineer with Gould Pumps. When he came home, he milked the cows and went to bed. On weekends he did farm work, and if he ever took a vacation day, it was to tackle some farm task that could not be accomplished otherwise. Rita's mother sewed all the children's clothes and, after the children were in high school, taught sewing and tailoring courses through the Cooperative Extension Service. Meanwhile, she raised everything the family ate: all the vegetables, all the fruits, the wheat for making flour, and the corn for cornmeal. She also kept chickens and pigs.

Looking back from an adult perspective, Rita sees her family's way of life as a conscious decision. "Even today, I don't think my folks will admit the extent to which it was a choice. It was verging on religion for them. Both my parents were the oldest in their families, and their younger sisters and brothers, on both sides, lived in town. My uncles and aunts lived regular lives. Certainly I saw this, and as a student in school, I saw that most of my classmates didn't make their own clothes or grow their own food. I realized that what I had grown up with was unusual, but as a child, whatever you grow up with is what you grow up with. You don't question it."

It seems fair to say that these early experiences form the warp of a life that has taken Rita a long way from Seneca Falls, New York, but not far from her roots. When she visited her parents recently, her mother found a doll's sweater that Rita had made at the age of six and gave it to her in a clear plastic frame. The tiny garment is quite complicated. The sleeves are shaped and have ribbing around the wrists. "I didn't play with dolls," Rita says, "but

I was supposed to, because I was a girl, and the only thing I could think of to do was to make things for them. I liked making shapes that fit together. There is a lot of neat geometry to clothing. It is interesting to take a flat piece of cloth and turn it into something three-dimensional."

At the moment, Rita's professional life as an editor of gardening publications is drawing her more toward plants than toward textiles. But on weekends during the winter, she travels all over the country giving spinning workshops. The public response is warm. "For so much of human history," she says, "everybody — men, women, and children — spent a lot of time with fibers in their hands. The fact that for a few generations now most people haven't is just a blip. Now, when people discover spinning, they feel as if 'this is where I belong. This is what I'm supposed to be doing.' I hear people say things like that all the time. They are expressing a real deep sense of having found something that feels right to them, something that's very satisfying."

She explains that the source of that satisfaction is physical. In the modern world, we have lost the sense of accomplishment that comes from using our hands. Spinners of yarn take this fluff and give it structure. As Rita puts it, "You're transforming a raw material into a useful product that you can knit or weave into cloth. The activity itself is very satisfying for most people — the feeling of the fibers in the hand, the contrast between the softness of the unspun wool and the strength of the finished yarn."

Wool is Rita's favorite raw material. Its natural shades are appealing in themselves, but she discovered that it was fun to dye the wool before spinning it into yarn. "You can get so many lovely colors from plants," she points out.

I was interested to learn that most plants are not dye plants. Of the 1,500 native plants in Connecticut and the thousands of non-native plants that can be grown here, only a hundred or so are at all useful for dyeing. Those that do contribute suitable pigments often work in mysterious ways. Sometimes you get very similar colors from very different plants. Rita grows three plants that yield a blue dye, and in each case, you would not suspect their hidden properties. The blue pigment is extracted from their very ordinary-looking green leaves.

"Woad, which is in the mustard family, looks kind of like a big leafy rosette of cabbage," Rita says. "It's a biennial, and its leaves produce a blue dye. A similar blue pigment comes from a tropical shrub in the genus *Indigofera.* I grow it from seed as an annual. It gets four or five feet tall in a growing season, with a woody, upright stem and lots of little pinnately compound leaves fluffing out on all sides. The third is a plant in the knotweed family, *Polygonum,* which looks like the knotweed that grows in ditches along the road. And its leaves produce that same indigo pigment that gives blue dye. All three plants can be grown here, and you can get lovely shades of blue from them."

Sometimes different colors can be obtained from different parts of a single plant. Rita gives the example of marigolds: the flowers yield colors in the yellow and gold range, and the leaves, greenish shades. But it doesn't always work that way. Black-eyed Susan flowers yield a dark olive green, while the leaves yield a bright gold. So the color you see in the plant is not necessarily the color you are going to get from the dye.

Rita goes on to explain, "Colors can often be modified by combining them with different treatments. In order to get the color to stick well on the fiber, you usually pretreat the wool or the yarn with one or another mineral or metal compound. The most common ones are compounds of aluminum, iron, copper, tin, and chrome. These are called mordants. You use only a tiny, tiny bit — it's like using baking powder when you're baking cookies. You can often get several different colors from one plant, depending on which mordant you use." It may be chemistry to Rita, but it is alchemy to me when purple basil gives a sea-green dye in an acid solution and brown in an alkaline solution.

In her first book, *A Weaver's Garden,* Rita wrote: "I was fortunate to study chemistry in high school and college with teachers who could explain the subject clearly and relate it to everyday life, and so I learned to think of chemistry as a practical approach to understanding materials and processes." *A Weaver's Garden* provides readers with the same sort of practical guidance conveyed in a most knowledgeable and engaging way. Each chapter focuses on a group of different plants traditionally associated with the crafts of weaving and textile-making and has a clearly written how-to section.

Rita's encyclopedic knowledge of plants and their secrets is the result of formal study, avid interest, and a wide range of experience with different plant groups. At Oberlin College, in Ohio, she majored in botany. "In those days, I studied plant anatomy and plant physiology," she says. "I learned about hormones, mineral nutrition and growth factors, and all the different things that are happening inside a plant, both physically and chemically. I also studied plant taxonomy, memorized the key traits of all the major plant families, and learned how to use a key to identify specific plants." She could have gone on to graduate school but wanted instead to work in the real world, and the best opportunity was in horticulture. "So I got a job in a nursery for a few years. The nursery was in Texas, and the plants were either greenhouse plants — tropicals — or the ornamentals that are hardy in zone 7 and zone 8, which was a whole different world from the natives in Ohio that I'd been studying. I was working with a completely different group of plants and working with them in a different way."

Then came the opportunity to spend a year in England, and Rita was off to a large family-owned nursery in Hertfordshire. While she was absorbing British nursery techniques, she also pursued another consistent interest — textiles. As a child of seven, she had been given a little loom, on which she wove her first scarf, but in junior high school knitting had supplanted weaving as her first love. At about the time she started college, her older sister Lois became intrigued with spinning. "I always wanted to do everything that she did, so I would stay with her quite a lot. This was in the early seventies," Rita explains. "At that time, no one we knew was doing any spinning, so we sort of invented it as we went along."

In England, Rita took one Saturday afternoon class in spinning, and that was enough to get her started again. "I made a real leap forward that year," she says. "The British are connoisseurs of wool and produce some of the best in the world." She found a book about the British breeds of sheep and traveled all over England, seeing the raw material on the hoof. "Different breeds of sheep are almost as different as breeds of dogs. You think of sheep as white, but a lot are black or charcoal gray or dark brown or a sort of rusty color. Wool can be short or it can be long; it can be curly or it can be fairly straight; it can be really, really fine or it can be quite coarse." She bought a variety of fleeces, and from that time on, spinning was an integral part of her life.

When her year in England was up, Rita returned to the nursery in Texas for a year or two, but with a new agenda: to start her own nursery, specializing in the native plants of Texas. However, it was an idea ahead of its time. In 1977, the surge of interest in using native plants in the garden was still a few years down the road. It was too soon for native plants and too soon for a single young woman to start her own business. Instead, Rita returned to graduate school to study botany.

"Horticulture is a great practical field," she says, "but as a science and an intellectual discipline, I found more challenge in botany. In particular, I was excited about ethnobotany, which is the study of plants that people use for one thing or another." She did some casting about for such a program and wound up at the University of Colorado, where she spent three years working on various aspects of ethnobotany. "I studied plant chemistry, which deals with things like the molecular structure of pigments used in dyeing and pharmacological compounds found in medicinal herbs." In ethnobotany, theory and practice came together in a satisfying way and led to an interesting project investigating the agricultural practices of the prehistoric Anasazi in the Southwest.

After that, an eighteen-month detour led to Costa Rica and research into the interaction between hummingbirds and the flowers they pollinate. While Rita claims her tour of duty in the cloud forests was "a lark," it was still within the realm of plant study. "It seems like I'd gotten off the track," she says, "but in fact this was all part of the track. Anyway, all these things ended up in a master's degree." It almost led to a doctorate, but ultimately, the do-stuff-with-real-things person won out, and Rita left the academic life behind.

She came home from Costa Rica when her visa ran out, thinking she would go back and get involved with tropical agriculture after she had "sorted some things out up here." But first she went to visit Steve Buchanan in Virginia, where he was teaching music at James Madison University. As Rita puts it, "We'd been friends forever, and it was so nice seeing him that we decided to get married."

In Virginia, Rita had a lovely summer garden, where she grew all the plants for her winter projects. She also had a job that she liked in the archeology lab at the university, studying ancient pottery shards found at Virginia Beach. "The pots themselves had been pretty thick and clumsy and crude," she says, "but they were marked on the outside with impressions of finely worked netting, cordage, basketry, and fabrics that had been pushed in while the clay was still soft. By studying these fragments of pottery, I was able to learn about the textile technology of the period."

At the same time she was happily doing the research for *A Weaver's Garden.* Then out of the blue she received a call from Connecticut. Would she be interested in joining the staff of a new gardening magazine with a practical, gardening-by-gardeners approach? Now a free-lance gardening editor, Rita looks back with some surprise at this turn of events. "Getting involved in gardening editing was just a fluke. It did not represent any thought-out career change, but as it turned out, here I still am. It's a checkered story."

Having known Rita and Steve since their arrival in the Northeast, I think otherwise. Like the fabrics she weaves, Rita's life has many different patterns, but it all grows out of the same natural thread.

The Seed Sowers

Please read this introduction before proceeding. The next two sections contain potentially dangerous information about seed sowing, which can be addictive.

All gardeners respond warmly to the magic of a sprouting seed. It never ceases to amaze me that a primula seed the size of a grain of pepper contains everything required to make not just any old roots, leaves, and blossoms but the specific roots, leaves, and blossoms of, say, a candelabra primrose. Candelabra primroses (*Primula japonica*) have thonglike roots, large rosettes of leaves, and tiered flowers on two-foot-tall stems. A bird's-eye primrose (*P. frondosa*), though, has sequin-size flowers on four-inch stems and a proportionally small root system, but arises from a similar grain of pepper.

When I discovered, thanks to a friend in the North American Rock Garden Society, that many species of primulas are easy to grow from seed, I entered a new phase of my gardening life. No winter goes by without my planting a few pots of primula seeds. But my modest activities are nothing to the herculean labors of the people you are about to meet.

Basically, there are two approaches to raising hardy plants from seed. As you will see, neither is difficult. Growing from seed can be as easy or as challenging as you choose. I am not adventurous. I like things that germinate easily and require no heroic measures. To me, life is quite full enough of challenges. When it comes to growing plants, I want cooperation. But this is not what real seed sowers are all about.

Many rock gardeners scorn the easy-to-grow. They love unraveling the secrets of seed germination. Maybe the seed has such a hard coat that it needs to be scarified — that is, you have to scar it by threatening it with a hammer or submerging it in water.

Stratification is another common procedure. It involves subjecting a seed to a moist, cold treatment in order to break its dormancy. I discovered that this can be done simply by planting the seeds in a moist medium in early winter and putting the pots outside in a shady place protected from drying winds. I put my pots under a lath roof on the west side of the garage. The seeds germinate in their own good time, just as they would in nature.

This is one method of growing from seed, and the easiest. Growing seeds indoors under lights is another. However, there are more steps involved in getting the tiny plants through the winter and into the garden. On the plus side, the indoor sower has the fun of watching over the seedlings.

In this chapter you will learn more about these two methods from skillful, compulsive seed sowers. And if you get hooked, don't say I didn't warn you.

Norman Singer and Geoffrey Charlesworth

In the fifteen years that I have known Norman Singer and Geoffrey Charlesworth, they have threatened every year to cut back on their winter seed sowing. And every year they have continued to plant approximately two thousand packets each. When I called Norman in April 1994 about this book, he announced that Geoffrey already had more than a thousand pots full of seedlings and more germinating every day. Not to be outdone, he reported that he also had a thousand pots. "This year, despite all our promises, resolutions, and swearings, we've sown more than we ever have before," he admitted. "A friend of ours says he knows a wonderful curse for us: 'May all your seeds germinate!'"

In his first book, *The Opinionated Gardener,* Geoffrey scoured the English language for words to describe a gardener in the grip of this insatiable craving to sow. He discarded "seedaholic" as clumsy and misleading: "It seems to describe a person inordinately fond of poppyseed pastry, halvah, or sesame-seed buns." He toyed with "greed," "addiction," and "passion," but pronounced them limited. Words like "ailment" and "affliction" also missed the mark: "It is no more an ailment than jogging to a high or collecting silver you have no intention of using. A disease? Certainly it is not infectious. Some people stand unmoved by packets of seed and rows of pots. Their only comment is: 'Whatever will you do with them all when they germinate?' If it is a disease, immunity is commonplace."

Norman and Geoffrey receive seed lists from dozens of plant societies, several commercial sources, three botanical gardens, and numerous amateur seed collectors. They used to hold a joint membership in each of the plant societies and endeavored not to duplicate each other's orders, but that didn't work. "If I read the seed list first and wrote down what I wanted," Geoffrey explains, "Norman would say, 'But *I* wanted that!' So I had to say, 'Well, go ahead and get it.' What we really want is to get our own things and not have to discuss everything we do with the other." As a result, they each belong to all the societies, and even their friends send them separate seed lists.

While the bulk of their sowing takes place in the winter, ordering the seed, entering their acquisitions in a notebook according to the donor, and logging that information into the computer takes time also. Their Czech friends start sending seed in October, and by December so much seed has arrived that they have a backlog of things to do. "Seed comes in all the time," says Norman gleefully. "We laugh and laugh because Lee Raden [a fellow rock gardener] says he sows his seeds on New Year's Day. How many seeds can you sow on one day? We're sowing all the time. We get annoyed if suddenly there is a blank day when nothing has come."

Sowing used to be done in the kitchen, where disputes arose over the use of counter space, but the addition of a greenhouse has solved that problem. As for their method, it is simplicity itself. Norman feels that if people knew how easy it was, everyone would be doing it.

The potting mix they use is half Jiffy Mix, readily available at garden centers, and half sand. Their sand comes from a local granite quarry and includes pieces of rock up to a quarter of an inch in diameter. They have it delivered to them in ten-ton lots, but a few buckets of any ordinary sand from the nearest gravel pit should do for beginners. To a large pail of their half-and-half mix, they add about a quarter of a cup of Osmocote, a slow-release fertilizer that is available commercially.

When the Osmocote has been well mixed with the potting medium, they fill small square pots, leaving a quarter of an inch of space between the surface and the rim. The seed is sown on top and a thin layer of fine gravel is sprinkled over it. (The gravel prevents raindrops from dislodging the seeds.) The pots are labeled and put in a kitty litter tray, to which water is added to a depth of about half an inch. When the top of the potting mix is damp to the touch, the pots are removed and allowed to drain. They are then put into flats (twenty-four pots fit snugly into a flat). And the flats go outdoors for the winter.

On the north side of the house are a dozen huge tables made with cinder blocks supporting long planks. The flats are lined up on the tables and covered. An inverted flat serves as a lid for each one. Perforations in the bottom of the lids admit rain but reduce its force. To keep the tops from blowing off, Norman and Geoffrey lay heavy metal garden stakes across them.

In the spring, forests of tiny seedlings emerge as the temperatures rise. When the time comes to transplant the seedlings, Norman and Geoffrey again use half sand and half Jiffy Mix. The abandon with which they sow is equaled only by their largesse. The vast majority of their seedlings wind up at plant sales to benefit the many plant societies to which they belong.

Besides the rage to sow and a consuming interest in plants, Norman and Geoffrey appear to have little in common. Norman is a New Yorker, born and bred; Geoffrey is from the north of England. Norman has a kind of blunt charm that is both endearing and intimidating. He is forceful and knows how to get things done. These qualities stood him in good stead during his tenures as the director of City Center, executive director of the Lincoln Center Chamber Music Society, and president of the North American Rock Garden Society. Geoffrey is basically a shy, diffident man who seems bemused at being caught up in the sociable, highly competitive world of rock gardening and rock gardeners.

In 1964, this unlikely pair bought a brownstone in New York City on what became a tree-lined street, thanks to Norman. He organized the block association and won an award from the Parks Department for his pains. "We were one of the first streets to plant trees," he recalls. "I was interested in that aspect of gardening, but Geoffrey was the one who started the garden out in back. Of course, you had to bring everything in from the street through the kitchen, and I was the bringer-in."

With Norman as undergardener and bringer-in, Geoffrey assumed the mantle of head gardener. At that time he was a professor of mathematics at Hofstra University, on Long Island, and commuted daily to his classes. But this happy state of affairs came to an end when he was made a dean and his schedule changed. In order to be near the campus, he moved out to Hempstead, and Norman inherited the city garden.

"I always loved it and was slightly resentful because Geoffrey knew more and therefore was in charge," Norman admitted while we were drinking tea one afternoon in 1994. "It is still that way," said Geoffrey with a sly smile. We all three laughed. Norman was prompted to tell the story of a new member of the Berkshire Chapter of NARGS who came up to him and said, "I can't keep you two straight. Geoffrey is the knowledgeable one, isn't he?"

For the record, Norman spelled out their respective areas of expertise. "In the garden, Geoffrey has always been the leader, because he reads more and works on it more. It's typical that when we were in the city, he was working on the garden while I was organizing the street association. He writes the book and I promote it." Whatever the dynamics of their relationship, it works, and it has worked for fifty years. They met in England during World War II at Bletchley, famous as the home of the "enigma machine" that cracked the code of Germany's military intelligence. Norman was with the American Army, Geoffrey with the British Foreign Office.

By the time their first garden behind the city brownstone became too shady for anything but bulbs, Geoffrey had a house and garden on Long Island. This house included a bit of woodland with azaleas and bird cherries, and he made a perennial border along the boundary fence. As yet there were no alpines. The tiny knobs, buns, tufts, and wisps of plants that set the hearts of rock gardeners racing are an acquired taste.

I was curious to know where and when Geoffrey's appetite had been whetted. Consulting his memory and Norman, he suggested that his inspiration might have come from a place near his mother's home in Newton Valley, a village near Sheffield. He remembered, "There was a bank right on the road. The owners had arranged it as a rock wall, with aubrieta and alyssum. It was much nicer than my mother's garden, which had asters, hydrangeas, and kniphofias — the big things." Norman remarked that the rock wall was probably the sort of thing that Reginald Farrer, the acknowledged father of British rock gardening, would have deplored, but Geoffrey defended it.

He became aware of American rock gardening by chance. One day, for want of anything better to do, he attended a flower show on Long Island. The local chapter of NARGS had arranged a display of stone troughs planted to resemble miniature mountain landscapes, and Geoffrey thought they were "super." Norman, in contrast, was scornful of plants so small that you had to crawl around on your hands and knees to appreciate them.

Today they both specialize in alpines, but unlike many rock gardeners, they love everything from the larger perennials to woodland wildflowers to shrubs and dwarf conifers. They even like annuals, and are quick to admit that these colorful single-season plants were among their first purchases for their present garden, in Sandisfield, Massachusetts. "At the same time," Geoffrey explains, "we had begun buying rock plants, but we didn't specifically make a rock garden."

The thing that amazes visitors is that they managed to find their property at all. In the southwest corner of Massachusetts, dozens of narrow, paved country roads wander through the woods with no apparent destination. Somewhere off one of these is an unmarked dirt road that makes a beeline to nowhere. Norman and Geoffrey own sixty-six acres on one side of this road and a house and twenty-two acres on the other, where their garden spreads southward and westward.

Ten years ago, an awestruck Robert Rushmore wrote for *House & Garden:* "Here, in fact, in a huge, plateaulike setting, growing in raised beds or in the foundation of a torn-down barn, is an astonishing garden for the student of plants. It contains a collection of over three thousand rock-garden plants along with a great variety of larger perennials, the whole interspersed with dwarf and weeping conifers and flowering shrubs, including many different kinds of rhododendron. Even more amazing, the garden is a little over a decade old."

It is now a little over two decades old and, if anything, more amazing. The achievement of two men who have passed their seventieth birthdays, the garden continues to expand. Norman and Geoffrey no longer fill their buckets of compost, soil, and gravel to the top; as a concession to age, they fill them only three quarters full. But they continue to tend the garden entirely themselves.

The plan or layout is a spontaneous reaction to the clear and present need for more places to plant their thousands of seedlings. The most formal element in this vast informal garden is a huge, partially paved square that matches the geometry of the house. The whole thing is mulched with pebbles, which gives it continuity, something that was not a priority for Norman and Geoffrey. The health and comfort of the plants was, and these plants like the sharp drainage provided by the stone mulch.

Geoffrey describes the evolution of this area: "I wanted a place to grow

cactus, and I built a raised bed. That was the first thing. Then we had a Czech guest who said, 'You need a crevice garden.' And he built one. Norman carted the rocks in a dump cart, Joseph [the guest] placed the rocks, and I filled in with soil mix. The crevice garden was in the middle of the lawn, which looked *awful.* So I made a place around it and joined it to my raised bed. Then I built another raised bed. I told Norman he could have a patch. And that's how it grew." Good-tempered rivalry notwithstanding, the allocation of space has been, according to Norman, "very amicable." "It's like colonialism," adds Geoffrey. "There is so much land, you just go where you want."

The need for more and more room is a direct consequence of the uncontrollable urge to sow seeds. No one has explained that urge better than Geoffrey, in *The Opinionated Gardener:* "There is no thrill so great as seeing a new species emerge from seed, produce its first leaves, and ultimately flower. By the time you have grown 2,000 species you could believe you have exhausted Nature's imaginative variability; by the time you have grown 5,000 you realize you never will. There is always something new." This is what Norman and Geoffrey's gardening is all about.

Christian Curless

It took exactly one winter to turn a normal, conscientious assistant editor at *Fine Gardening* magazine into a man possessed. Chris Curless met his downfall in the line of duty. New at his job, he was put in charge of the department called "Tips." Readers are urged to share their innovative solutions to common problems with fellow gardeners, and the best tips are published. Being a thorough, hardworking young man, Chris felt compelled to try the suggestions sent in by contributors.

"This tip was just sitting there in the file," he recalls. "It was for a homemade light box for starting seeds. It looked pretty straightforward, so I decided to build it." The materials were readily available: a four-by-eight-foot panel of rigid foam insulation board covered with foil; duct tape to hold the top, sides, and ends of the box in place; and one double shop light with two cool white fluorescent tubes. He found that he could slice up the insulation board with a Swiss army knife and that the construction took only about two hours.

Chris set up the finished light box in his basement and soon had dozens of little pots basking under the fluorescent tubes. Six feet long, eighteen inches wide, and sixteen inches deep, the box has no lid. Instead, it rests upside down on a table of Chris's devising: an old door supported by two milk crates. One long side of the box is hinged to the top and lifts up to allow access to the interior. The lights are attached to the underside of the top. And that is really all there is to it.

Now in its fifth winter, the light box has been a complete success. Initially the long side flap was hinged with duct tape, but repeated opening and closing eventually wore out the tape, and Chris replaced it with hinges. Other than new fluorescent bulbs every year or two, no upkeep is needed. With the lights on and the flap closed, the interior of the box is ten degrees warmer than the rest of the basement. It creates a cozy, draft-free environment for germinating seeds, and later for the seedlings. Since you have to kneel beside the box for an eye-level view inside, creature comfort is provided by a thick pad of foam rubber on the floor. "That cement floor is so cold, it sucks the heat right out of your kneecaps," says Chris cheerfully.

On a recent Sunday in February, we knelt side by side like communicants while he reverently lifted the long side of the box. A good many of the small plastic pots inside contained plants already showing their true leaves. Other pots were still covered with plastic wrap to maintain even moisture for germination. All were carefully labeled in Chris's tidy, minute printing.

"A couple of these are things I got from Chiltern's in England," he said, picking up the pots one by one and studying the labels. "This is *Plectranthus ciliatus.* I really have no idea what it's going to be. This I sowed yesterday — *Gaura lindheimeri.* It's supposed to take dry conditions, and I thought it might do for my front bank. This is *Nepeta sibirica,* which seems to be an up-and-coming plant. And these are *Salvia argentea.*" Two pots were full of tiny furry plants. "From day one, as soon as they put up true leaves, they're covered with these little wooly hairs. I collected the seed from plants I grew myself, and I love them. I love the silvery foliage." The last pot was sown with *Chasmanthium latifolium,* an ornamental grass that takes shade.

"That's what's cooking at the moment," Chris went on. "I just got my twenty-five packets from the North American Rock Garden Society the other day. What I'll do is fill up the light box. Then, when I run out of space here, I'll take certain plants that tolerate some shade and put them upstairs on the south- and west-facing windowsills."

From the look of the seedlings, the game of musical pots was about to begin. The light conditions are not perfect upstairs, and the small plants strain toward the sun, but Chris turns the pots every day. As soon as the nights are warm enough, he begins acclimatizing them to the outdoors, a process called hardening off. As he explained, "I harden them off on this little mini-porch that faces east. In the early spring about half to two thirds of the porch is in shade. So I'll start them at the back corner and then move them down to the front of the steps. The steps eventually get full sun."

If you think it all sounds like a lot of work, it is, but consider this. Over a period of four winters, Chris has grown from seed as much as one half of the plants in his garden. For a young couple with two small children and all the expenses of owning a house, growing from seed makes sense. "I haven't felt I could buy a lot of plants, and that's why the seeds have been important to me. I can't go and make a plan on paper and say, 'Yeah, I'm going to go out and spend five hundred dollars,'" Chris said. "But I'm relatively patient, so I've done some shrubs and a lot of perennials. I'm just kind of waiting for them to come along. My notion is to try to put together a pool of plants. Then one of these days I'll rearrange them in a garden."

The first year he had the light box, he started with about fifteen different kinds of seeds. It was a motley collection. He swapped seed with a colleague at *Fine Gardening* and bought other varieties through seed exchanges. And he was elated when about 75 percent germinated. "I really found that this was a lot of fun. The next year I did a whole lot more, and the next a whole lot more than that. I don't know what year I peaked, but in 1992 I started about eighty different kinds." Not all the seedlings survive the transition from light box to windowsill to porch to garden. As Chris notes, "The real hurdles are hardening them off and getting the perennials through that first year out in the garden."

Be that as it may, an impressive number of plants have emerged from the light box in the basement. Several excellent woody specimens have found their way into my own garden: a sturdy little oakleaf hydrangea (*Hydrangea quercifolia*), a beautiful *Pieris floribunda,* the native andromeda with upright clusters of small white bells; an eastern redbud (*Cercis canadensis*), and innumerable annuals, most notably a wonderful ornamental pepper with nearly black foliage and fruit that turns from purple to red.

In his own garden, Chris has begun a homegrown shrub border. Handsome, well-established rhododendrons (*Rhododendron carolinianum*) are among his successes, along with the hydrangeas, andromeda, and *Rosa glauca*. The rhododendrons on the north side of the family room are the backbone of a shade garden in progress. As for perennials, seed-grown *Aruncus dioicus,* Siberian iris, and *Geranium sanguineum striatum* are all beginning to make a show. Even by his own critical standards, "*Aquilegia alpina* was fantastic from seed, very vigorous."

During the winter months, while his seedlings follow their own vegetative timetable, Chris dreams and plans for their future deployment in the garden. The Curless property has more garden space than any other house on their street, one of the reasons they bought it. Mature trees have gobbled up many of the lots, which are fifty by one hundred feet, but theirs has an extra plot on the north side of the house, the site of the shrub border and shade garden.

Assessing his progress to date, Chris says, "At the moment, I have lots of little collections. In some cases, I'll have a spot and just jam in a plant. I've got a lot of different kinds of plants. Now I'm about ready to think about a real plan. I want some more themes. I'm trying to figure out what's really feasible, especially on a small property. What I need to do here is use more annuals and try to have different gardens do their things at different times. I have lots of little gardens, and I think that can work. As long as you don't ask every garden to look good all the time, then you're okay. If my little rock garden in front is only colorful in spring, that's fine. Maybe the one along the foundation should be for summer into fall. I need to do that sort of thing."

While Chris never imagined that he would make any branch of horticulture a career, he always had a hankering to be a home gardener. Even as a child growing up in Arizona, he fancied gardening. "I did big impressive vegetables, the sort of thing that gets a kid going — watermelons, cantaloupes, cucumbers," he remembers. "With a little bit of water, the cucurbits just went berserk, and that was a lot of fun. I guess I always kind of remembered that. When we moved to Miami Beach, I had a vegetable garden. After that, I got very heavily into academics in high school and just didn't have time for gardening." But the seeds had been sown.

At the College of William and Mary, in Williamsburg, Virginia, he studied history and French and wondered what to do next. "In my senior year, a friend said that New York University had this French studies program and that I should give that a try." That led to employment with the French-American Foundation, but at the end of a couple of years, Chris was no closer to finding a career that suited him. However, he was still young enough "to get away with jumping tracks entirely."

His plunge into horticulture was a complete break with family tradition, which had produced three generations of physicians. Chris himself says, "You've got to wonder." The remembered pleasures of growing plants surfaced out of nowhere. "There really was no reason for it, except that being in New York, I was beginning to feel kind of hemmed in," he says. "Also, I wanted to do something a little more meaningful to me than just working in an office. It was at that point that I decided to pursue gardening in a serious sort of way."

That way was paved by his former employer. "My old boss at the

French-American Foundation had gotten married and moved to Norfolk, Connecticut. One of the people she and her husband met up there was Fred McGourty, and they got him to do a garden for them. She told me that Fred was somebody I should talk to. So one day in February I went down to the New York Botanical Garden, where he was giving a lecture. We met, and he offered me a job on the spot. It turned out that my former boss had an apartment in Norfolk that Lynn and I could rent at a reasonable rate, so we decided to make the leap."

Chris worked for the McGourtys at Hillside Gardens, their perennial nursery, for two years. "I learned huge amounts there," he says. "In fact, that was my gardening foundation. All you have to do is go up there in the summer and see what they have done in that space. It's pretty remarkable — the sheer variety. And the plants are beautiful. It was a great place to learn."

Later, when a position at *Fine Gardening* opened up, it seemed too good an opportunity to pass up. Chris's three and a half years there rounded out his horticultural education. "Because the Taunton Press approach was to find somebody knowledgeable and get them to share their story, you'd end up working with the authors and learning what they knew. So that was a great experience," he says.

In the meantime, he had become an avid gardener at home, which was what he had wanted all along. "We rented a house in the summer of 1991 and then moved here in April 1992. So we've been here three full summers. It's nice to have garden-related work during the week," he says. "But I really live for weekends and playing around here on my own time."

Lynn, who appeared with the two children — Sarah, age three, and Jeffrey, six months — asked if I wanted her editorial comment. I did. She shook her head and said, "What this man does is kind of unbelievable."

For Show

To American gardeners, "the greatest show on earth" is not the circus. It is the Philadelphia Flower Show. Produced by the Pennsylvania Horticulture Society and held annually since 1829, it is certainly the oldest and probably the most distinguished flower show in the United States. I have always attended and enjoyed the New York Flower Show, which is handy to my Connecticut home and never fails to lift my spirits with heavenly smells of damp earth and fragrant spring bulbs. But my first visit to the Philadelphia Flower Show was a revelation. While comparisons are odious, they are also inescapable. I was completely bowled over by what greeted me at the Philadelphia Civic Center.

It was 1988, and the show's theme that year was "The World Is Your Garden." A stop-you-dead-in-your-tracks archway of orchids welcomed visitors at the entrance to the vast hall. Orchids seemed a fitting choice to express the theme, as they can be found everywhere from the Connecticut woodlands to the rain forests of South America and represent the largest of all flowering plant families, with 25,000 species. The arch, which spanned an opening as wide as a three-lane highway, was constructed of bamboo and covered in moss. Every inch of the moss was studded with sprays of tiny orchids, thousands of them, in a medley of lovely colors: pale pink, magenta, yellow, orange, chartreuse, and white.

Having barely recovered from the floral rainbow over my head, I was confronted with a jungle bower where more orchids festooned the gnarled branches of moss-encrusted trees. A rich understory of palms and ferns went down to the edge of a pool traversed by a graceful red Oriental bridge. The six-thousand-square-foot exhibit, "Rendezvous in Singapore," was created by the Singapore Tourist Promotion Board and Singapore Airlines as part of the central feature. Half a dozen other major exhibitors contributed to this display. An additional thirty-odd horticultural businesses, nurseries, and plant societies filled the remaining six acres of the Civic Center with individual gardens boasting forty-foot trees, full-scale buildings, decks, terraces, gazebos, and more plants than you could possibly imagine.

There was an eighteenth-century European garden with pink and white hollyhocks, lavender foxgloves, plumes of pink astilbe, and white shasta daisies massed against a background of arborvitae. The structural elements included a garden folly, beautiful fencing, and latticework, all painted a soft cream as a neutral background for the eight-foot delphiniums and beds of 'Bonica' roses.

Ten pages of my garden notebook catalogued the other wonders that I saw that day. I was entranced by local garden-club exhibits and wrote at length about the "rooms" from around the world. Ditchley Park was my favorite. The back wall and short side wall suggested a room in the English country house where Churchill purportedly escaped from the pressures of government. The walls were covered in deep red watered silk, and an Oriental carpet in rich shades of red and blue defined the floor space. The great man's easel stood facing the viewer. In front of it was an old wooden chair made more comfortable with a squashy, much-patterned cushion. A magnificent bouquet of fresh tulips and stocks posed on a pedestal for the absent painter and filled the canvas on his easel. The rest of the room was furnished in handsome English oak. Over the sideboard, where a brandy decanter and glass stood ready on a small tray, an ancestor brooded from a heavy frame. This exhibit had already been judged and had been found "Perfection."

Equally fascinating were the miniature settings, the Defined and Open Space classes, and the Niche Class. While I loved everything, I had no idea what went into the preparation of these exhibits. In short, I was ignorant about the wonderful world of flower shows. It wasn't until I began to think about gardeners in winter that vivid memories of these marvelous displays came to mind. I knew then that investigating this exciting branch of gardening was a must. Through the garden grapevine, I found Pinkie Roe.

Pinkie Roe

From New Year's Day until after the Philadelphia Flower Show, Pinkie Roe's dining room in Mendenhall, Pennsylvania, looks like a church basement before a tag sale. Assorted props litter the sideboard and dining table, along with a welter of leaves, twigs, dried flowers, stones, seashells, raffia, and scraps of material. During the winter of 1994, the clutter included fishing nets, whole coconuts, and a huge piece of coral. The theme of the flower show that year was "Islands in the Sun," and Pinkie had just returned from the Caribbean. She had been snorkeling off Belize when she spotted the coral washed up on the beach.

"I thought, 'My God, that looks just like the Philadelphia Flower Show!'" she explained to me. "You always keep the exhibition-worthiness of things in mind, and when you stumble on them, you just grab 'em.'" Grabbing a brittle fan of delicate sea coral three feet across was not easy. Nor was getting it home. But Pinkie was determined not to abandon her prize. She wrapped it in a large plastic garbage bag and cradled it tenderly throughout the trip. The coral changed planes three times and arrived home in one piece. There in the dining room, it underwent a metamorphosis. Set on a piece of driftwood and bedecked with orchids, it became the centerpiece for Pinkie's entry in the Room & Table Class.

Exhibitors in this division of the competitive classes stage their entries on platforms that are eight feet deep and ten feet wide. An eight-foot-high wall serves as a backdrop. Displays of this size are usually done by an organization or a club, and a modest subsidy is provided by the show's sponsor, the Pennsylvania Horticultural Society. With her friend Alberta Malloy as cochairman, Pinkie got together a small committee from the Delaware Center for Horticulture to work on the project.

All the classes have titles, which come out of a brainstorming session conducted by the show's organizers, members of area garden clubs, and other exhibitors. Pinkie, who has been in on meetings of this sort, told me the rationale: "We try to come up with evocative titles that don't dictate the style of the design. For instance, we would avoid saying 'a line design,' because it's kind of restrictive. We try to make it so that anything goes."

Exhibitors are allowed to interpret the titles in any way they choose. Given "Island Fare" as the rubric for the Room & Table Class that year, Pinkie's group set a picnic table with green Mexican glass plates and a fishnet tablecloth. They decorated it with conch shells and, as the *pièce de résistance,* the fan of coral embellished with fresh orchids.

Like the piece of coral, the picnic table had a history. "One spring it floated up the Potomac River and landed on my father's property in Virginia," Pinkie explained. "He hauled it up from the river and was using it as a potting bench. It's the worst-looking beat-up old thing you ever saw. But it was perfect." To add verisimilitude to the island vignette, members of Pinkie's committee spread five hundred pounds of oyster shells to surface their beach scene. Their ingenuity was rewarded on this occasion with a second place in their class and a red ribbon. What delighted Pinkie as much as anything about their success was that the display cost so little. "It was fun, because everything was either begged, borrowed, or stolen," she said.

By the time Pinkie had retrieved her props from "Island Fare," she was already thinking about the next year's show. Entering a display in the Philadelphia Flower Show is almost as competitive as the event itself. While the current show is still in progress, the organizers announce themes and classes for the following year. The moment entry forms are available, hopeful exhibitors fall on them and rush to get them in the mail. Even so, in the case of the most popular classes, acceptance boils down to the order in which the applications are received.

As I write, the 1995 flower show is still a month away, but Pinkie, who is an old hand at getting her applications in promptly, has been at work for weeks. This year she has entries in the Defined Space Class, the Niche Class, and the Miniature Arrangement Class, as well as an important part in the Garden Club of Wilmington's project for the Garden Class.

There are two major areas of competition: the design, or artistic, classes and the horticultural classes. Pinkie, who competes in the design division, describes how these classes are structured, starting with the Defined and Open Space classes. "These are in the individual exhibitor section and involve smaller spaces than either the Room & Table Class or the Garden Class. The defined spaces are enclosed by walls and measure seven feet high by six feet wide by four feet deep. They look like a department-store show window. The open space is just a platform four feet square, with no sides. There are four entries in each class. My friend Susan Detjens and I are in one of the defined spaces this year. The title is "Snip It, Clip It, Dig It," and it's supposed to feature garden tools. We're thinking of having a wheelbarrow as part of the design . . . and some vines."

A niche, in flower show parlance, is a lighted box with a framed opening. Niches come in three sizes: large, with an opening thirty-four inches high and twenty-six inches wide; medium, twenty-four by twenty inches; and small, twelve by ten inches. "I have niches out in the shed, niches of all sizes," says Pinkie. "And what happens is that from January on, the dining room is turned into sort of a workroom. My husband is terribly tolerant and lives with this mess until March. It's just awful. There's always something being mocked up. Sometimes in the kitchen as well."

Although Pinkie has recently become tempted by larger spaces — "It gives you a little more elbow room and a little more scope" — she still enjoys creating diminutive designs. Entries for the Miniature Arrangement Class have to be made of dried plant material and must not exceed five inches in any direction. These arrangements are displayed at eye level in shadow boxes with framed openings eight inches square.

The most ambitious displays by amateurs at the Philadelphia Flower Show are those entered in the Garden Class. In this class, there are always four competing gardens. However, the requirements vary each year. The 1995 exhibitor's handbook gives the following guidelines: "A garden from the past, present or future interpreting a benchmark in design, horticulture or cultivation technique. To be staged in an area 20 feet by 20 feet with two 10-foot walls provided by PHS [Pennsylvania Horticultural Society]. Architectural appointments, fresh-cut flowers and accessories permitted."

To conceal the bases of balled-and-burlapped plant material, the garden display area has sides, like a giant sandbox, and the PHS supplies exhibitors with mulch and sod as needed. Because the installations are labor-intensive and involve substantial production costs, garden clubs rather than individuals undertake these exhibits, and the PHS contributes a hefty subsidy, which the clubs match. Pinkie loves a big project like this. "Putting in a garden takes manpower, a lot of hauling around, good old wheelbarrow pushing and dirt moving, so we'll have at least a dozen or fifteen workers," she says.

When I visited her during the summer of 1994, Pinkie and members of her club had been working on their entry for the 1995 Garden Class for months. The garden they were planning was based on the plant discoveries of Ernest Henry Wilson, or, as he is better known to admiring gardeners, Chinese Wilson. To this intrepid plant hunter we owe the introduction of innumerable garden treasures from the Far East, including the regal lily (*Lilium regale*), Kurume azaleas, the rare and beautiful dove tree (*Davidia involucrata*), the familiar and aptly named beautybush (*Kolkwitzia amabilis*), and many species of *Malus, Prunus,* cotoneaster, viburnum, berberis, rhododendron, and maple — to mention a few.

Like so many creative ideas, the inspiration for a garden of Wilson discoveries came about during work on another project. A few years ago, the Garden Club of Wilmington entered the Container Class with a replica of a Victorian conservatory. Pinkie recalls the following chain of events: "I was the chairman that year, and my friend Susan Detjens was the vice chairman. Susan is a very accomplished artist and a very creative person. Anyway, she was down at the University of Delaware library doing a little research on Victorian conservatories when she ran across this book on Chinese Wilson, which mentioned all the wonderful plants that he had introduced. We thought it would be fun some year to base a garden on his discoveries, and it turned out that it fitted in with the theme for the 1995 flower show." That theme was "Moments in Time: A Galaxy of Gardens."

To my astonishment, Pinkie produced a professional rendering of the proposed design, complete with groundplan and elevations. I learned that the skilled designer of the garden was one Peggotty Gilson, a member of the garden club who had always wanted to be an architect. "She's our age, and women weren't expected to have careers when she was young," Pinkie said. "They were expected to marry and have children, and she did. She was an artist and did drawings of people's houses and of their children and their pets, but that wasn't really what she wanted to do. So she decided to go back to school."

Before Gilson could get into architecture school, she had to take remedial classes in math. She stuck to it, and to the admiration of her friends she became a full-fledged architect. Although her career now precludes participating in many of the garden club's activities, she produced renderings of a delicate Oriental-looking pavilion and a reflecting pool, a Lutyens bench flanked by large porcelain pots against an elegant screen, and, in the four corners, beds of trees, shrubs, and ground covers.

Describing everyone's role in the project, Pinkie says, "Peggotty was the architect, Susan was the artist, my friend Molly Wiley was the business manager, and I was the teamster and cheerleader." Susan was also the primary researcher. She came up with the required statement of intent, a rough draft of which read: "This idealized garden showcases some of the 1,500 plants introduced from Asia by Dr. E. H. 'Chinese' Wilson during the period 1899–1920. Still used today, these trees, shrubs, vines, perennials and bulbs have also provided the breeding stock for new generations of plants."

Lining up nurseries to furnish the plants and guarantee their out-of-season bloom makes the show a real cliffhanger. One year the club wanted witch hazel for their design. "The person we tried to get it from said it would be over by the time of the flower show," Pinkie says. "So we ordered a crab apple instead, and it was forced two weeks too early. It was shot, and we couldn't use it." On this occasion there was a happy ending. The club was able to get its first choice from a local nursery, one that has plenty of experience forcing plants for the show.

As members of the Garden Club of Wilmington, as individuals, and as a team, Pinkie and Susan are no strangers to blue ribbons. They belong to what the former describes as "a sort of hard core of about half a dozen of us in the club who are the flower show jocks." For the club's 1994 Garden Class entry, they really cleaned up. "We got a lot of silver that year," says Pinkie. "It was wonderful."

Although she always participated in her club's flower show projects, it wasn't until about a dozen years ago that Pinkie first entered as an individual exhibitor. "I was very familiar with putting in entries as a member of the garden club. We'd done rooms and tables and gardens. But I'd never thought about entering on my own. Then one year after I had finished being chairman of a couple of these Room & Table projects, Molly Wiley followed me as the flower show chairman. She looked at the schedule and said, 'There's a class for novices in the arrangement section. You've got to enter this class.' So I looked at the class, and I thought, 'Yes, I could do that, and also this and this.' So I ended up entering three classes, and I've been in it deeply ever since."

Gardening runs in Pinkie's family. The present headquarters of the American Horticultural Society was formerly the home of her paternal grandparents, and both her parents are interested in gardening. "It's just something that we've always done," she says. "We lived seven miles down the river from my grandparents and were back and forth a lot. In fact, when

I was little — I am the eldest of six children — one of the things I loved to do most was sometimes to go and spend the night with my grandparents by myself. And I would help my grandmother in the garden. That was her big thing. She worked right along with the gardeners and was very involved in it all."

Pinkie's mother, whose nickname is spelled Pinkey, has always loved gardens too. She is still a horticultural judge for the Garden Club of America. However, she began her career as a dig-in-the-dirt kind of gardener. "I'm a firm believer," she says, "that to show 'em, you have to grow 'em. I think the two go hand in hand." Her own parents had a beautiful garden in Washington, D.C. "Mother didn't dirt-garden, as Pinkie and I have done, but she was very artistic, so I think we've all inherited a little of that talent from her."

Over the years, Pinkey Matheson, like her daughter, became increasingly interested in the design and arrangement aspect of flower show competition, though she insists that Pinkie has far outdistanced her in that department. Nevertheless, this shared enthusiasm has given them both pleasure, and they have enjoyed taking courses together. "One year we went to England for a week to study with Sheila McQueen," Pinkey told me.

Pinkie picked up the story. "Sheila McQueen is absolutely the grande dame of English flower arranging. She's just wonderful. She arranged flowers for the royal weddings and lives in a charming village, where she still gives classes. She also lectures extensively and is usually in the United States a couple of times a year. I know she's in her eighties. Actually, she's just my mother's age. And it's so reassuring to see that flower arranging is one of those things that you just get better and better at. Age doesn't slow you down in the slightest. She's quite remarkable and an inspiration."

The two Pinkies are also an inspiration and quite remarkable.

Cut and Dried

You have met winter gardeners who leave their gardens outdoors and those who bring their plants inside, roots and all. Others leave the roots in the soil and bring in the aboveground parts of the plants. Cutting and drying herbs and flowers for winter use is an ancient practice. Until quite recently, any useful plant was considered an herb, and herbs have been employed for thousands of years and in thousands of ways — medicinal, culinary, domestic, and ritualistic.

Botanists once doubled as doctors, and vice versa. In the first century A.D., Dioscorides, physician to the Roman Army, taught himself to be a first-rate botanist. He had to be. Plant parts were the only remedies available to his patients. Medieval monks carried on the tradition of treating sickness with herbal medicines, and in the New World, colonial housewives brewed "simples" from their gardens to restore the ailing.

Traditionally, herbs and spices livened up dreary food and took the curse off rotten meat, disguised unpleasant smells and warded off diseases. Plant parts also served as building materials and yielded fibers for textiles. Plants' oils were distilled and used in everything from perfume to furniture polish.

As decoration, dried plants were brought indoors as early as the eight-

eenth century, and the ceremonial use of fresh-cut evergreens goes back to the Golden Age of Greece and further. It is only in the past hundred years that we have lost touch with plants as an integral part of everyday life and a vital ingredient in special occasions.

Recently there has been a rebirth of interest in plant lore and crafts. The gardeners in the next two sections have participated in this renaissance. What better time than winter to rediscover the uses of dried herbs and flowers?

Betsy Williams

Having just discovered the Proper Season, I mourn its recent closing. Until a few months ago, it was a fascinating craft shop devoted to herbs and flowers. As herbal crafts are one of the most attractive and consuming of winter occupations, I knew that the shop's owner, Betsy Williams, would be just the person to interview for a chapter entitled "Cut and Dried."

The shop was located in a cul-de-sac off a side street in Andover, Massachusetts. At the back was a charming little garden paved with gravel and enclosed with a plank-and-lattice fence. A few small tables and chairs invited patrons to linger in the shade of a huge maple tree. Ivy filled narrow beds at the foot of the fence and twined around the base of a stone birdbath. Color was provided in the spring by pots of pansies.

This was where Betsy staged the seasonal celebrations that made her shop such a lively, engaging place. At Christmastime, the gravel would be covered with straw and the walls draped in evergreens. Festivities included carols, refreshments, Christmas stories, and a visit from Saint Nicholas. In May there was a Faerie Festival, complete with faerie punch and faerie cakes, minstrels, and music.

The shop offered dried flower arrangements and wreaths, elegant topiaries of dried plant material, potpourri mixtures for special occasions, and books on herbs and flowers. The handmade wreaths were described by one publication as "works of art." But the shop was only the tip of the iceberg.

Betsy, who is the author of several booklets on herbs and their meaning, is also a member of the International Herb Growers and Marketers Association and a member of the British Folklore Society. She has contributed chapters to two best-selling herb books, *The Pleasure of Herbs* and *Herbal Treasures,* and is presently working on a book about potpourri. A brief author's biography in *A Wreath of Christmas Legends* states that "herbs and flowers, their lore and history, are Betsy Williams' business and her passion."

She also lectures about all aspects of herbs, leads trips to herb gardens, and teaches classes and workshops in herbal crafts and herb gardening. Herbal galas are one of her favorite activities. "I'm good at producing events," she says. "And I love doing it. I love things with a tidy beginning, a tidy ending, and a fabulous crescendo, like weddings and seasonal events — the Christmas program and the Faerie Festival. At the shop, we used to do the Saint Nicholas celebration outdoors in candlelight."

Weddings are and will continue to be a major part of Betsy's business. They are always a source of pleasure. "When I do a wedding seminar," she says, "I'll get ten people from all over the country to spend four days learning wedding work with fresh herbs." Although she loves dried herbs and flowers, she no longer has time to make wreaths and arrangements. About four years ago, she turned this work over to her friends and helpers of many years, Joan Moore, Victoria Anderson, and Renate Schott. But Betsy does all the weddings. Prospective brides and their families come in droves to the Williamses' comfortable old colonial house to pore over photographs of bouquets, nosegays, centerpieces.

Weddings are as much a family affair for the Williamses as for their clients. Betsy's husband, Ned, a free-lance graphic designer, creates beautiful cards that explain the meaning and symbolism of flowers and herbs. He also designs personalized wedding invitations with herbal and floral borders.

Betsy provides another service: the preservation of keepsake flowers. Brides from all over the greater Boston area bring their wedding bouquets,

Rita Buchanan spins in her greenhouse during a snowstorm. Bougainvillea, powder puffs of red *Calliandra haematocephala*, and a hanging basket of Christmas cactus surround the spinner with living color.

Rita dyes her fleece with roots and flowers from her garden.

A colorful collection of conifers graces
the winter garden of Norman Singer and
Geoffrey Charlesworth.

The rippling, twiggy branches
of *Salix* 'Golden Curls' are
set off by the dark barn siding.

Geoffrey (left) and Norman work companionably
but separately in the greenhouse.

The installation of the Garden Club of Wilmington's
entry for the 1995 Philadelphia Flower Show was
an enormous task.

The Proper Season's holiday window box contains
winterberry, boxwood, juniper, and pine.

Betsy Williams assembles Christmas decorations in her workshop. Flowers and greens for wreaths and dried arrangements hang from the beams.

Left: This wreath made from dried plant material contains lemon leaf, cockscomb, yarrow, roses, statice, and pomegranate.

Opposite, top: In the loft above the workshop, the temperature is between 90° and 110° Fahrenheit, optimal for drying.

Opposite, bottom: Snippings from the workshop show the range of plant material suitable for drying.

The Proper Season's holiday window box contains
winterberry, boxwood, juniper, and pine.

Betsy Williams assembles Christmas decorations in her workshop. Flowers and greens for wreaths and dried arrangements hang from the beams.

Left: This wreath made from dried plant material contains lemon leaf, cockscomb, yarrow, roses, statice, and pomegranate.

Opposite, top: In the loft above the workshop, the temperature is between 90° and 110° Fahrenheit, optimal for drying.

Opposite, bottom: Snippings from the workshop show the range of plant material suitable for drying.

Deirdre Larkin entwines a candelabrum with variegated holly
and ivy, both classic Christmas greens with a long history.

and Joan, Victoria, and Renate dismantle them, dry the flowers, and reassemble them as haunting souvenirs. "Once the flowers have dried, we use them to create a wreath or an arrangement in a basket, or else I'll make them into a potpourri," says Betsy. "We always add statice and baby's breath and sometimes a few more dried roses or carnations to fill out the design."

This appealing work is carried out in the barn workshop that the Williamses built fourteen years ago. It is an enchanted place — rustic, flower-bedecked, and deliciously scented. From the rafters hang bunches of yarrow, statice, baby's breath, berries, seedpods, and greenery. True myrtle (*Myrtus communis*), which holds its lovely fresh color when dried, is the most important of all wedding herbs. They use so much of it that they have to order it from California by the case. I learned that myrtle has been associated with Aphrodite, the Greek goddess of love, and Venus, her Roman counterpart, since preclassical Greece. Aphrodite was often depicted carrying a sprig or wearing a crown of this shrubby evergreen. A small tree in its Mediterranean homeland, it is also a popular subject for topiary, with its tiny rich green leaves and compact twiggy habit.

It was in the course of drying wedding bouquets that Betsy and her staff learned that even fragile blossoms like sweet peas and lilies can be preserved. "Most garden material will dry, one way or another," says Betsy. "And it can be quite fascinating. Americans never used to like the subtle, monochromatic schemes using interesting dried materials. They wanted things that were bright and shiny and looked real when they were dried. But Europeans, particularly Germans and Scandinavians, appreciate material that has a softer, antique look. Now, thanks to *Victoria* magazine and its misty camerawork, Americans are loving what we came to call 'dead flowers.'"

I was stunned by the range of flowers that Betsy uses: amsonia, miniature daffodils, larkspur, stocks, sunflowers (the "in" flower of the moment), ivy, mimosa, bridal wreath, all different kinds of roses, delphiniums, buttercups, blue salvia (she grows her own and also buys it), chamomile, pansies, zinnias, gladioli, bells of Ireland (which turn a lovely parchment color and hold their intriguing shape), lichens, sweet woodruff, and thyme. Woodruff air-dries nicely and holds its green well. A few, like pansies, are fragile and tend to reabsorb moisture.

Natural air-drying takes place on the first floor of the barn; air-drying with heat occurs in the loft overhead, where the dried wedding bouquets are stored in white cakeboxes. "We heat with a coal stove, and Ned stokes it at five o'clock every morning," Betsy explains. "You need it hot — between ninety and a hundred and ten degrees, but no hotter than a hundred and ten. Quick drying is what you are aiming at. Every plant changes color as it dries, but some, like delphiniums, hydrangeas, and yarrows, hold their garden color. Roses are another story. A red rose turns black. But you can take an orange rose, and it turns bright red. The lavender roses, like 'Sterling Silver', 'Tiffany', and 'Heather', turn an incredibly marvelous claret, just gorgeous. Some of the pinks will deepen, and whites turn a soft, creamy yellow. But the yellows don't dry well at all."

When Betsy began her business, she grew most of the plant material in her own garden. At that time, she spent the summer growing, picking, harvesting, and drying. Creating the wreaths and arrangements occupied the months from September until Christmas. But when the dried flower business became a year-round proposition, she had to buy flowers to dry. She and her staff stockpile dried pepper berries from California and cases of dried blue salvia from Vermont. Seasonal things she gets fresh from the Boston flower market and dries them on the premises. Now her chief year-round occupation is to keep everything running smoothly. This fact makes her wistful.

"I wish I had time to do more writing," she says. "I love lecturing, I love doing research, I love traveling. That's why I love winter so. It gives me a chance to do these things. The rest of the year I'm too busy. Starting in the spring with the weddings, weekends are fully booked. And the staff — I love the people, but I hate the book work. I don't want to spend the next twenty years doing bookkeeping. I want to spend them reading fabulous books, learning more about gardening — there is so much I don't know and so much to learn. There's this banquet out there, and I have to keep saying,

'Gee, I can't have another course because workman's compensation has got me on the phone."

All of the foregoing, plus the fact that Betsy and Ned work an eighty-hour week, explains their recent decision to make a change. In the newsletter they publish twice a year, Betsy wrote, "The time has come for us to relocate, both the business and ourselves. For many years I have wanted to live nearer the ocean. I grew up on the ocean and I miss it. Ned spent all his boyhood summers in Maine and still loves the coast of Maine. We have often talked of finding a piece of property on the Maine coast where we could live and have the business. We've decided now is the time to do it."

In that issue, they announced the closing of the shop. The good news for clients, customers, and local friends is that everything else will be business as usual while they are looking for a new home. The old yellow house on Chestnut Street will continue to be the place where weddings are planned; where, in Betsy's office off the kitchen, the phone rings constantly; where the kitchen is always full of visitors and anyone is welcome.

The hospitable Betsy invited me to breakfast. We sat at a wonderful old pine table under a low ceiling. There were plants on the windowsill above the kitchen sink, and strawberries twined up a trellis on the wallpaper. Between interruptions, Betsy sketched in the background of a successful business career and a long, satisfactory marriage. I learned that both her parents were writers. Both were also much married, with several different partners each. Curiously, Ned's mother and father showed the same inclination to marry often and temporarily. But Ned and Betsy broke with family tradition. Their enduring union is now in its thirty-sixth year.

"I'm the opposite of all these young women today," says Betsy. "When I hear that this is the first generation of women to have worked, I want to take them and rap them on the side of the head and read them their history. My mother was a professional woman, a writer and a librarian. She was thirty-six when I was born, and she had a good career in back of her when she married and had children. She did a biography of Mary Mapes Dodge, which she finished the year I was born. She had a fine professional reputation and was in *Who's Who in American Women.*" As a child, Betsy did what her grandchildren are doing today: she grew up in private day care or was supervised at home by housekeepers.

Betsy's father was also taken up with writing. He contributed the section on farming to the 1963 edition of the *World Book,* having already written an important history of American agriculture called *Billion Acre Farm.* His twenty-three other published books were on history and the American West, but he also loved growing things. Betsy remembers that wherever he lived, he always had a garden. She also had an uncle in New York State who was an avid gardener, but she did not begin gardening herself until she and Ned bought the property on Chestnut Street. By that time, they had three children and not a lot of money.

"I wanted to be an at-home mother," she says, "but we needed extra income." She had always adored fresh produce, so she began by growing vegetables for sale and for home consumption and found it fun. "For years I grew practically everything we ate. I canned and kept three freezers filled. When we moved here, the gardening instinct that had been latent in me just germinated and popped out. It was a combination of having the property and, of course, the kids.

"I've told this story so often that my poor children groan. But you see those two dusty shelves in the window right there?" We were still at the kitchen table, and next to it, sun was pouring in across the plant shelves. "Well, Ned put those there so that I could grow the plants the children and I were reading about in the Beatrix Potter books." Many were flowering plants, but there were also herbs, which sent Betsy in search of information about growing herbs indoors. "I bought a book by Adelma Simmons, of Caprilands, and that did it! I got so taken up with the whole thing that I couldn't stop. I was hooked forever. I also started growing plants that I found interesting from a historical point of view."

Another book, *An 18th-Century Garland,* by Louise Fisher, aroused her interest in dried flowers. A chapter entitled "Winter's Pleasant Ornaments" reminds readers that dried flowers for decoration are part of our heritage. When Betsy set out to explore the realm of suitable subjects for drying, she was as original as she was daring. "It's not all cut and dried," she says, "any more than a flower is cut and dried. No two flowers are alike. Every one is unique, and you just have to figure out what method works best for that flower. That's part of the fun for someone with an inquisitive mind."

There are, however, certain rules. "If you are drying in silica gel, you always cover your container. If you're drying in another one of the desiccants, such as kitty litter, sand, or borax, you never cover. You have to know a little bit about all the methods. Try them out and see which works best."

All the strands of Betsy's life came together in the Proper Season — her love of growing things and of history, her interest in research, and her skill with words. Above all, herbs and flowers gave her an opportunity to exercise her talent for working with people. And it is this aspect of the business that she enjoys most. She loves people and refuses to take a dim view of the human race.

If you have raised three children, lived energetically, worked hard, managed your own business, and reached the age of fifty-five, you have met both the up side and the down side of life. Certainly Betsy has done all these things. What she and Ned have not done is watch a great deal of television. "It's not because we are intellectual snobs," she hastens to explain. "It's just because we usually have so many other things to do." But during the Winter Olympics of 1994, the Williamses found themselves spending more time than usual in front of the television screen. They were genuinely shocked at the seemingly commonplace violence they saw on both the news and the regular programming.

This led Betsy to wonder if their lives had been unusually sheltered. She thought not. She and Ned had recently returned from a trip that had taken them all over the United States. They hit the road in February 1993 and returned home that November. They drove, flew, and bused around the country, staying in motels, in the homes of strangers, and with friends. They met and talked to all kinds of people, most of them involved with herbs, flowers, or gardens. From this experience, Betsy gained a perspective that she shared with readers of the Proper Season newsletter:

"Is it possible that people who work with plants are kinder, gentler and more caring than other people? If so, then we all have a mission. We might even be able to change the world! As plant people and gardeners, let's share what we have learned by living with our plants and gardens. Let's be open-handed and open-hearted with our love and enthusiasm for all green growing things. Let's get the world growing! Plant a garden, patio pot or window box. Teach a child to garden. Grow extra plants and produce and give them away to interested people. Celebrate the seasons and teach others to, also."

Deirdre Larkin

Deirdre Larkin has always loved Christmas. She and her husband collect old-fashioned glass ornaments from Germany and enjoy trimming their tree. She garlands their New York City apartment with holly, ivy, and evergreens. Until the winter of 1990, she thought of these preparations as a pleasure, not as a profession.

Cut to 1994 and imagine Manhattan at Christmastime. It is a "gridlock alert day" in midtown. Traffic is at a standstill, and horns are blaring. Tourists stand three deep in front of decorated store windows and clog the sidewalks. Meanwhile, grim-faced office workers buck the human tide to reach their steel and glass cubicles.

Not far away, at the Cloisters, a branch of the Metropolitan Museum, the atmosphere is hushed and reverent. Devoted to the arts of the Middle Ages and looking for all the world like an ancient monastery, the Cloisters stands on a bluff high above the Hudson River. Thanks to the foresight and generosity of John D. Rockefeller, Jr., who gave the land and the money to construct the museum, no high-rise mars the view of the Palisades. Towers and arcades roofed in terra-cotta tiles and gardens enclosed by original stonework give the building a feeling of total authenticity. Within, portions of several medieval churches and chapels have been skillfully incorporated into the overall design. Visitors, even restless schoolchildren, fall under the spell of these architectural paeans to the glory of God.

In a workroom across the cobbled courtyard from the Fuentidueña Chapel, Deirdre carefully binds fresh bay leaves one by one into a tapered swag. "What you have to do to get this classical swelling in the center is start from the middle and go first to one end, then the other. You do a continuous wrap, using individual stems," she says. Each garland represents ten hours of work, and when all four are finished, they will festoon the Italian altar canopy, or ciborium, in the Langon Chapel.

These bay leaf swags have been faithfully copied from a thirteenth-century fresco depicting scenes from the life of Saint Francis of Assisi. Just before Christmas in the year 1223, Saint Francis paid a visit to the little town of Creccio. After celebrating the Christmas mass, he knelt before the altar, where a replica of the Christ Child lay in a manger. Miraculously, the holy child came joyously to life before a group of awed onlookers. In the fresco, they stand behind and on either side of the kneeling saint. Overhead, bay leaf garlands hang gracefully between the four pillars of the altar canopy.

According to Deirdre, the garland as a form of decoration was popular long before the Middle Ages. "It is exactly the sort of thing that you find in Greco-Roman art. The bay tree and the palm were both associated in ancient times with victory, and they were adapted as Christian symbols very early in the history of Christianity. The idea of using bay laurel to crown a victor corresponded to the idea of Christ as the victor. Being an evergreen, bay laurel was also associated with immortality. A lot of the Christian plant symbols definitely draw on Greco-Roman tradition or European folklore, but they are modified and Christianized."

Part of Deirdre's job description is "researcher/coordinator responsible for the design and fabrication of historical seasonal decorations." And she loves her work. "It's such a funny occupation to have in this day and age —

garland maker. People think I'm crazy," she says with a serene smile. "But I like it. My friend, the conservator, is great at it too, because she is used to working very slowly and methodically."

In addition to mounting the seasonal displays at the Cloisters, Deirdre's responsibilities include assisting in the planting, maintenance, and interpretation of the gardens and giving lectures for the Saturdays at the Cloisters series. For a young woman with a master's degree in medieval religious history and a love of plants, whose favorite occupation as a child was making May altars, the position is tailor-made. "I sometimes think the reason I have such a feeling for the ceremonial use of plants has to do with my old-fashioned Catholic education," she says. "A lot of emphasis was placed on symbolism and meaning. We still had processions and crowned the Virgin and decked ourselves out with wreaths and garlands."

The May altars were the best part of all. The children collected every blue and white flower they could find and made elaborate decorations in honor of the Virgin. "No one does it anymore, but they were still doing it when I was a child," Deirdre says. "I realized after working here, this is probably as close to making May altars as you can come." Her laughter sounds delighted but slightly embarrassed. It isn't often that work affords someone pure, childlike pleasure.

Although Deirdre grew up in New York City, she used to spend summers in the Catskills, where several members of her mother's family shared an old farm. From earliest childhood, she loved roaming the fields and collecting wildflowers, which she and her siblings pressed or made into potions. She explains, "The property in Delaware County was owned jointly by Mother and her sisters and their husbands, and my grandmother sort of presided over the place. She was a great gardener, and in the last ten years both my sisters and my brother have turned into gardeners. So obviously, the seed was there. We all did it at about the same time."

Deprived of her own plot of land, Deirdre was prompted by her love of gardening to visit the New York Botanical Garden, where she enrolled in the certificate program. When she completed the course, she stayed on as a part-time gardener. "I was working at the Botanical Garden and also at the Dyckman House museum, the last Dutch farmhouse in Manhattan," she says. "But I was desperate to work at the Cloisters. My field was medieval studies, and I had been coming here since I was a little girl. The Cloisters was my absolute dream job."

The sequence of events that resulted in the dream coming true began with a phone call. She learned that the garden staff at the Cloisters was very small and that any opening in the near future was unlikely. But horticulturist Susan Moody asked if Deirdre would be interested in volunteering her services. "That was in the spring of 1990. I called her that November and said that I would like to volunteer. And that's how I began doing the Christmas decorations. When Susan found out that I gave garden tours at the Dyckman House, she asked me if I'd be interested in doing garden tours here. Soon after that, one of the staff left, and she called me."

Having had a close brush with academia, Deirdre considers herself lucky. "I like to use my hands as well as my head," she says. "The trouble with academic life is that you find yourself getting into topics that are so recherché only you and five other people in the world are interested in the subject. Other people haven't the faintest idea of what you are doing or why. Whereas you come to the gardens at the Cloisters and *everybody* understands what you're doing. People's response to plants is immediate. Here, I get to work out in the garden with the plants, and I get to lecture and do research."

When she was given the assignment of researching medieval Christmas decorations, there were two main thrusts: to make them as authentic as possible, and to make them safe for the artwork. Formerly, the ciborium in the Langon Chapel had been wreathed with Della Robbia–style garlands combining fresh citrus fruit with greens. Deirdre says, "It was discovered that the acids from the fruit were actually pitting the medieval stone, plus we had wire up against the columns, which was causing nicks and abrasions. The bay garlands that we use now haven't any resins or fruit acid, and we figured out a way of supporting them by weights so the stone is not affected. We fill little felt bags with fish weights — sinkers. Then we put the ends of the garlands into niches in the ciborium and weigh them down with the bags."

Both plant symbolism and the ceremonial use of plants fascinate Deirdre, who hopes one day to write a book on the subject. "There's nothing very comprehensive out there," she says eagerly. "Of course, a lot has been written about the nineteenth-century language of flowers, but it hasn't been very thoroughly researched. You really need to go back to the sources — that's what I would love doing. You need to go back and work it out."

Finding the Saint Francis frescoes with authentic period Christmas decorations was a real coup. "In the frescoes, Saint Francis is saying the mass at an altar under a ciborium that looks almost exactly like our ciborium, and it is garlanded for this Christmas mass with bay leaves. So that was bingo!" Deirdre explains. "But it was a rare instance. I would love to have more evidence like that. For the rest, I'm deducing that these plants were used. I may have some clues as to how they were used but no concrete representation, and I'm inventing."

She took her evidence where she could find it. She delved into account books from churches and monasteries and was gratified to find records of exact sums spent on holly and ivy to decorate the church. Old English carols were another useful source. "Most of the carols were recorded in the fifteenth century, but they contain much older matter. And they draw on liturgical plays and folklore. Some of this stuff is really pretty ancient," she says.

"The bay garlands that we use on the ciborium come from a different tradition altogether. In the Christianizing of Europe, you have both the old pagan indigenous traditions being assimilated into the church calendar and the traditions coming out of the Greco-Roman world. The bay garlands that you see in Roman art and all through the Renaissance come out of a different cultural complex from the holly and the ivy."

According to Deirdre, one of the things that happened when Europe was Christianized was that many of the old festivals, such as the harvest festivals, broke away from their original places in the calendar and became attached to the ecclesiastical holidays. Thus, many of the traditions associated with harvest festivals gravitated toward Christmas. In the fifteenth century, wheat, which was originally a symbol of harvest plenty, began to appear in paintings of the Adoration. Another Christmas custom involving wheat was instituted by Saint Francis, who urged people to "throw grain and corn upon the streets, so that on this great feast day the birds might have enough to eat, especially our sisters, the larks."

In terms of suitable plant material for the Cloisters, wheat filled the bill from both a historical and a practical standpoint. It was dry, harmless to the artwork, and long-lasting. For the past two years, one of the most impressive seasonal decorations has been Deirdre's gigantic wheaten wreath, which hangs from the ceiling of the Romanesque Hall.

With the exception of wheat sheaves, Deirdre could find no evidence of dried plant material in use as decoration before the eighteenth and nineteenth centuries. "We like dried material for the shapes and colors. But in the Middle Ages, people were more interested in meaning than in form," she notes. "The meaning of the plant was inherent in its being alive and green. So I like wherever possible to use fresh greens."

In the main entrance hall she has a freer hand in choosing decorative material, because the archways are made of modern stone. Here she can use fresh greens, which she does with an inspired and lavish hand. In the great garlands over the entrance arches, she embellishes the greenery with fruit, nuts, and rosehips. "These are my babies," she says. "What I do is put the greens on frames out in the workshop." When the workmen have installed the frames over the archways, Deirdre climbs fearlessly into the bucket of a cherry picker to attach the decorations.

I asked about the significance of the apples and discovered that they were part of an ancient harvest custom of wassailing the orchard trees. To promote a good apple crop the following year, people treated the trees to songs and encouragement in the form of little cakes hung from their branches and cider poured over their roots. "That's one of the folkloric traditions that gravitated toward Christmas," Deirdre says. "With the hazelnuts there was a similar tradition. Iconographically, both apples and nuts appear in paintings of the Madonna and Child."

Finding concrete justification for the use of rosehips proved more difficult. "There is a really prominent use of rose symbolism in carols," says Deirdre. "There are also numerous stories about roses blooming miraculously at Christmastime. But there is a distinction to be made between plants that came to have a symbolic association with Christmas in art and plants that might actually have been used. Obviously the rosehips wouldn't still have been viable at Christmas. So they are a more poetic use."

As there is no distinct line between what Deirdre does for enjoyment and what she does for employment, historic and symbolic decorations are as much a part of Christmas at home as at work. When photographing at the Cloisters presented insurmountable problems, she invited Karen Bussolini to come to her apartment on Fort Washington Avenue. The Christmas tree had already been trimmed, evergreen swags hung from the moldings, and the foliage of variegated holly and ivy wreathed a handsome candelabra.

"There is something profoundly satisfying to me about what I do," says Deirdre. "I think it's because it connects with my childhood love of all this sort of thing. While I love plants and gardens and making decorations, I always like it when there is a little bit more than an aesthetic rationale. I like it all to mean something. I am really hooked on the symbolic aspect of it."

Getting Together

The most popular winter sport among gardeners is not skating or cross-country skiing; it's hanging out with other gardeners. Although twenty years of teaching eroded my tolerance for meetings and name tags, I willingly attend numerous garden gatherings, duly labeled and glad to be there. My winters would certainly be the poorer without the North American Rock Garden Society's annual Winter Study Weekend.

This event is held on both the East and West Coast and attracts the *crème de la crème* of gardeners, both as speakers and as members of the audience. It is regularly attended by as many as three hundred like-minded souls, among them professional growers and nurserymen, botanists, and modern plant hunters. Passionate amateurs are well represented, and beginners are welcome.

You don't have to be an expert to enjoy the company of other gardeners and to learn from them. Plant societies and garden groups come in all sizes, configurations, and levels of expertise. I also belong to the American Hemerocallis Society, and the daylily people are the most inclusive and democratic of gardeners. Their motto is "the more, the merrier." Anyone can play.

Nor are bylaws necessary for an exchange of ideas and camaraderie. For years, a friend of mine who lives in New Hampshire has been meeting once a month during the long northern winter with three other gardeners. Quite apart from the pleasure she derives from their company, she finds that "it helps to have friends. They push you along and you push them." Every year they investigate one new genus.

In the vicinity of Boston, a somewhat larger group gathers four times during the winter season. Called the Hardy Plant Study Group, it has an informal structure and a simple purpose: "to help us know more about a wide range of plants by sharing our knowledge of the literature about the plants and our experiences growing them." The brief statement ends with the warning that "we intend to meet only *out* of the gardening season." For each Sunday afternoon meeting there is an organizer, and the event takes place at a local public library. Last winter this studious band concentrated on *Astilbe, Heuchera, Aconitum,* and *Tiarella.*

Betsy Williams of the Proper Season told me about a little group in Marblehead, Massachusetts, where she used to live: "I had a friend there. I've lost track of her now, but she and her neighbors formed a club. They were all avid gardeners, living on the same street and at home with small children. They needed something in the winter to keep their spirits up, so they started the Root and Radish Club. By the time they presented themselves to me, they were all well along in years, but all five of us were gardeners. That's how we got to know each other."

Recently I learned that two friends of mine were joining forces once a week to study woody plants. Living too far away to participate, I've found a kindred spirit in my neighbor Martha McKeon. We had the initial meeting of our Shrub Club at her kitchen table. For the occasion, I provided a jeweler's loupe with which to scrutinize bits of *Chamaecyparis* she had clipped from the display garden of the nursery where she works. We consulted reference books, looked up other species and cultivars, and had a delightful time.

Another informal group that gave me enormous pleasure while it lasted was the Pipsissewa Society. The young man who formed the group has gone on to bigger and better things, but for several years the meetings brightened many a winter afternoon. Gary Keim, a graduate of the Professional Gardener Training Program at Longwood Gardens, arrived in Connecticut at age twenty-six, knowing no one. In short order he tapped into the garden grapevine and before long had friends and contacts galore. He was one of my passengers on a spontaneous nursery field trip. After that, half a dozen of us spent much of that summer visiting gardens, exchanging plants, and comparing notes.

Long before the first snow fell, Gary began fretting about the dreary New England winter. He was afraid of losing touch with his newfound garden friends. "That's how I got the idea of the plant group. I thought it would be fun to meet once a month, see slides, and share ideas," he said. As for the name of the group, pipsissewa is the common name of *Chimaphila umbellata,* a small native plant with whorled evergreen leaves. It is a familiar woodland plant throughout the Northeast and a favorite of one of the other members. A third thought the word "society" had more class than "club." And that is how the Pipsissewa Society was born.

To start a study group, all you need is another obsessed gardener or two and a plan — you have to decide when and how often to meet and what to discuss. Beyond that, the requirements are simple: a kitchen table with a good light; some reference books; stacks of nursery catalogues (everybody should bring his or her favorites); and a notebook. The jeweler's loupe is useful; a slide projector is optional; and a plate of cookies or other sustenance is essential.

If do-it-yourself groups don't appeal to you, join a plant society. The fourth edition of Barbara J. Barton's wonderful sourcebook, *Gardening by Mail,* lists 246 different special-interest groups. The choices begin with the African Violet Society of America and end with the American Willow Growers Network. There is something for everyone. In this chapter, you will meet David Burdick, who belongs to an unusual group in Pittsfield, Massachusetts.

The Springside Greenhouse Group

David Burdick and I first met in 1992 at the Berkshire Botanic Garden in Stockbridge, Massachusetts. He was the horticulturist there, and I had given a talk about primroses. We found shared interests in the genus *Primula* and in woodland gardening, and discovered a less likely bond: David was born and brought up in the same small Connecticut town where I had grown up a good many years earlier.

After that, we saw each other at rock garden society meetings. We also had mutual friends, from whom I learned that David was involved with a community greenhouse. When I called him about this book, he invited me to come and see how he and the Springside Greenhouse Group spend the unsung season.

While David was working at the Berkshire Botanic Garden, several members of the Springside Greenhouse Group came to help out as volunteers, and friendships were forged. Later, when he joined the staff of Windy Hill Nursery in Great Barrington and found himself with nowhere to winter over his tender plants, an invitation to join the group was forthcoming.

According to David, the membership is large and varied. As he says, "It runs the gamut from people who can just spell the word 'plant' to very experienced gardeners." And their interests are equally diverse. The greenhouse, which belongs to the city of Pittsfield, is old and for that reason appears a bit rundown. But inside, spirits are high, and so is the level of maintenance, which is a communal effort.

When I arrived on a weekday morning in mid-March 1994, half a dozen gardeners were at work on their plots. Val Myers, a native of Germany and a member since 1978, told me that she had been attracted to the group by the idea of a "working garden club." Her friend Nina McDermott mentioned some of the special interests represented: "Somebody may grow all herbs; somebody else may be involved in bonsai — you'll look around at their plot and that's all they have. David's plot is very different — the bromeliads. That's something unusual that we haven't had before. What's fun is that you get to learn from each other. Of course, a lot of people have what I refer to as a mutt plot. That's what I have — a little bit of everything — a couple of these, and a couple of those."

I asked these two women how often they visited their plots. Val said, "Oh, I'm here at least once a week, probably two or three times a week now that it's March and everything's growing. Some people come once a week, others come once a month. But somebody from the watering committee comes every day so that even people who can't come as often as we do have their plots taken care of. It's quite organized."

Nina added, "There's also a spray committee that controls insect problems. Then there is a committee of three or four people who raise the plants for our plant sales. The city obviously doesn't have any funds to give us, so we have to make sure we generate enough money to support ourselves. We have a plant sale in May and another, smaller one at the end of March." Both agreed that it was a real joy to come to the greenhouse in the winter and see everything in bloom.

The large main greenhouse, where the members have their three-foot-square plots, is thirty feet wide and sixty feet long. At one end is a small, rather shabby meeting room; at the other, a potting shed equipped with fluorescent lights, where members can start seeds. Consideration for fellow seed sowers must be exercised, and when the seedlings reach a certain size, they have to be moved out to the greenhouse plot to let other members have a chance. The lights are set on an automatic timer, twelve hours on and twelve hours off.

Beyond the potting shed are two smaller greenhouses. These provide club space for growing the plants for the annual sales. But in the spring, the smallest one is opened up for members to purchase additional plots to accommodate the overflow of seedlings. (David usually has designs on one of the extra plots.)

The remarkable thing about the Springside Greenhouse Group is that it has been functioning, with very few hitches, for nearly thirty years. It was the brainchild of Carl P. Deame, a remarkable horticulturist whom I knew slightly in the late sixties. At that time I was a neophyte gardener and he was superintendent of Mrs. Bruce Crane's Sugar Hill Nursery in Dalton, Massachusetts, just outside Pittsfield. On my first visit to the nursery, I was beguiled by some gorgeous, extremely expensive standard rosemarys that Deame had lovingly clipped and trained as perfect topiary pompoms. He noticed me admiring his handiwork and assured me that I could make my own. On the spot, he picked out a small potted rosemary cutting, whipped off the lower leaves, and handed it to me. He told me not to touch the growing tip but to keep shortening the side shoots. In a couple of months I was back with my ugly duckling, which in a flash he transformed into a respectable if immature standard rosemary.

I was charmed to learn that the same Carl Deame had organized the Springside Greenhouse Group and was responsible for starting several working garden clubs in the area. Springside Park overlooks the town center and, in the distance, the Berkshire hills. More than 80 acres of the 230-acre park were given to the city of Pittsfield by the Miller family. Kelton B. Miller, the editor of the Berkshire *Evening Eagle,* donated the first parcel of land in 1910. His two sons later gave another large parcel in memory of their father. This came complete with a Victorian mansion and greenhouse.

In the fall of 1968, Deame drafted a proposal to use the greenhouse as winter quarters for his garden group. He and his colleagues presented their case to Vincent Hebert, then the parks commissioner. According to a report issued by the secretary, "Permission was not long in being granted, especially in the face of such a unique and worthwhile project." On Wednesday, September 18, the first meeting of the Springside Greenhouse Group took place to draw up bylaws and general guidelines. Now retired, Hebert is still an honorary member. "They're an excellent group," he says. "And they have done wonderful things for the city of Pittsfield."

Of necessity, the size of the group was, and still is, limited, based on the number of plots available in the greenhouse. These plots include the space above and below the raised platform on which the plants are grown. A note in the rules and regulations states in capital letters, "YOU DO NOT RENT THE AISLE OR ABOVE IT." You can, however, have up to four hanging pots above your plot, as long as they do not cut out the light for other people's plants.

Plots and keys to the greenhouse are issued upon payment of dues, which are used to defray the cost of heating — the biggest expense — and to pay for supplies such as potting soil, limestone, peat, superphosphate, and fertilizer. Pots can be purchased on the honor system. David explains how it works: "There is a little box with everybody's name on index cards. You pull out your card, write down what you take, price it — there is a list right there — and then you settle up at the end of the year. It's just a service to the members."

The group is fortunate to have people like Bill Loucks, who has been coming almost every day for years. He is in charge of building maintenance. When the temperature falls below forty-five degrees, Bill's home phone number is automatically dialed. He explains, "I have a message on there that says, 'You'd better get up to the greenhouse, because the temperature is below forty-five.'" Once the furnace went off and the temperature fell to thirty-six degrees. Fortunately, the heat had failed toward dawn, and solar warmth soon helped raise the interior temperature.

The watering committee is crucial to the survival of the plants, and indeed to the success of the group as a whole. "With a cooperative venture like this," says David, "you make arrangements so that each person on the watering roster will only have to come up here once or twice a month. My day is Sunday, and we have three other people who water on Sunday, so I only have to come up once a month." However, for his own pleasure, and for the sake of his plants, he comes far more often.

His plot stands out because of the curious, dramatic-looking forms of the epiphytes. He introduced me to *Neoregelia,* the fingernail plant from Brazil. In its natural habitat, it draws sustenance from the organic matter and water that collects in its rosette of leaves.

His tillandsia, with a magnificent fan of pink bracts and purple lily-flowers, won first prize in the group's 1994 show. "It's very different from the so-called atmospheric tillandsias, which are grayer in color and look like something from outer space," he says. These he grows in three tiered kitchen baskets. The plants live on humidity and a daily spritz of water, which then drains through the wire mesh baskets. "I think they're great plants — they're so sculptural. I really enjoy them," he declares happily.

David showed me other specialized plots. "Here's Harvey's space. He belongs to the Rare Pit and Plant Council, which deals with growing plants from organic matter left over from dinner." We moved on: "There is an interesting plot over here. It's Sue Haddad's. She's been a member here for about three years. She's also involved in a group called Connections, a community support program for people with psychiatric disabilities. Sue has done a lot of work with them up here, and she's got them organized into a workforce. They had a big party a while ago to clean up Springside Park."

We looked at the bonsai corner. "There are about five or six guys in this group who are really passionate about bonsai, and from time to time they organize their own little study group within the group. The bonsai plants do well up here because they get a light watering every day, and that's exactly what they require."

As I took leave of my guide that day, I thought of the group's founder and mentor, Carl Deame. The Springside Greenhouse Group has done him proud.

Reflection

It was a year ago, almost to the day, that I drove up to Pittsfield to meet David Burdick at the Springside Greenhouse. The weather was raw and the roads slushy. It was the tail end of winter and the beginning of this book. I have learned so much during this year.

From Joanna Reed, I learned about "backing into work." There is often a point in writing a book when you think that it can't be done — that it is too much. But I recalled Joanna's woodland after the twister, strewn with litter and fallen trees, and I pushed on. I have thought of her nearly every day this winter. Occasionally I have phoned her — always waiting until after dark, when she will have come in from the woods.

I have spent these winter days in such good company that I hate to let them go — the people in this book. Mary and Dick Kordes sent me a video so that I could see their garden in all seasons. I have heard the frogs on their pond in the spring and watched the moon rise through the winter trees. I've seen the first snow of the year, and the second, wet and weighty. I've followed Dick on his snowshoes through the firs. He even threw a snowball in my direction.

A week ago, Dodie Freeman won first prize and an impressively large rosette of blue ribbon at the Philadelphia Flower Show. The award was for her display in the Miniature Arrangement Class. In the eight-inch-square framed opening, a single shelled hazelnut rested on a base the size of a penny. One shield-shaped eucalyptus leaf rose to a point behind the rounded form of the nut kernel, and behind that, in perfect proportion, two tiny iris blades finished the composition. The background had been painted burnt orange, a tone that complemented the russet skin of the hazelnut. Curiously, the minute arrangement had the impact of a large bronze sculpture viewed through the wrong end of a telescope. It was wonderful.

Pinkie Roe's garden club worked night and day for weeks, building the elegant structures for Chinese Wilson's garden, their exhibit in the Garden Class. I wanted them to win a first place. The design was serene and beautiful and the idea both interesting and educational, but the judges were looking for something else. Who knows what? That's flower shows. Pinkie met me at the Philadelphia Civic Center the day after the show opened. "Come to gate eleven at seven-thirty on Sunday morning," she said. She took me over every inch of the six-acre site. For her, it had been a grueling week, but you would never have guessed. That's gardeners.

June and Jack Dunbar sold their house the day that Karen Bussolini took the photographs for this book. The winter jasmine was in full bloom, as were blue pansies. Jack always tried to have something in flower every day of the year. He will find Litchfield County winters more of a challenge, but perhaps bloom won't be his focus. Perhaps it will be a calligraphy of bare branches against a backdrop of snow. Whatever the new direction, it will be passionate and precise.

Karen and I have conferred throughout the unsung season. "What is blooming in your window?" I ask. And she tells me about the fuchsia cutting I gave her and the bulbs that are sprouting. She has loved the winter people as much as I have. I am still poring over her photographs, vicariously delighting in everything she saw and seeing anew through her eyes and lens.

The days are getting longer. Despite a recent cold snap, the snowdrops are in full bloom. I have finished this book, and it is time for spring.

Appendix

Selected Readings

Index

Appendix

Karen Bussolini and I hope that the photographs and text have whetted your appetite for more information about plants and activities that make winter a pleasure. The following annotated lists are intended to provide practical guidance. These lists are the handiwork of several people. Karen, who particularly loves birdwatching, compiled the list of winter food plants for avian visitors. My friend and neighbor Martha McKeon, a wonderful gardener with nursery and greenhouse experience, helped with the list of plants for winter beauty, indoors and out. And the people interviewed alerted us to their favorite books on specific subjects, supplied us with suggestions about plants, and offered advice about their special interests.

The lists are arranged in the order of the subject matter in the book.

Inner Resources: Selected Plants for the Indoor Garden

Abutilon (parlor maples): Bushy plants with crepe-paper bells in many colors. A south-facing windowsill in a cool room suits these profuse bloomers. Cultivars:
   'Clementine' — rich red flowers
   'Moonchimes' — dwarf plant with yellow blossoms
   'Snowfall' — plentiful white blossoms
   A. megapotamicum 'Variegatum' — with gold-mottled leaves and yellow flowers

Alocasia watsoniana: A handsome foliage plant with trim, arrowhead-shaped leaves veined in white. Alocasias need warm temperatures, not below 65° F.

African mallow (*Anisodontea hypomandarum*): Wonderful for windowsills; a long season of bloom from pink flowers.

Begonia aconitifolia (angel-wing begonias): Great favorites of the Martin family. Cultivars:
    'Pinafore' — frilly leaves, salmon flowers
    'Tom Ment' — silver-speckled foliage and coral pink flowers
    'Orange Rubra' — a favorite for hanging baskets, with orange flowers
    'Orpha C. Fox' — compact enough for a windowsill; silver-splashed leaves and pink flowers

Begonias (fibrous): Easy to please in bright light and temperatures above 60° F. Cultivars:
    'Firmament' — leaves of pink, silver, and bronze
    'Looking Glass' — glistening silver leaves
    'Midnight Sun' — green, cream, and pink leaves with white flowers

Camellia japonica: Thrives at temperatures from 36° to 58° F; suitable for a cool greenhouse. Beautiful, but fussy about temperatures.

Clivia miniata: Tovah Martin describes this handsome amaryllis-like plant as "close to unkillable." (When my husband and I bought our house thirty-five years ago, a clivia came with it. We still have it.) Gorgeous clusters of yellow-centered orange flowers, dark green strappy leaves.

Ferns: The following are Melitta Collier's favorites.
    Maidenhair fern — *Adiantum* cultivars
    Autumn fern — *Dryopteris erythrosora*
    Boston fern — *Nephrolepis exaltata* 'Bostoniensis'
    Nephrolepis exaltata 'Hillii' — majestic fronds with forked, ruffled leaflets

Fuchsia 'Honeysuckle': Highly recommended by Joy Martin for its year-long bloom. Elongated orange-red bells. Cool night temperatures suit it.

Carolina jasmine (*Gelsemium sempervirens*): A vigorous vine with yellow trumpet flowers. Blooms all winter.

Florist's broom (*Genista canariensis*): Covered with small yellow pealike flowers in late winter. A favorite of Sarah Milek's. Prefers cool night temperatures.

African violets (*Saintpaulia*): Familiar and popular for warm houses.

Jasmine (*Jasminum polyanthum*): A vigorous vine with masses of sweet-scented, starry white flowers.

Palms:
    Lady palm (*Rhapis excelsa*) — a compact palm resembling bamboo
    Fishtail palm (*Caryota mitis*)
    Chinese fan palm (*Livistona chinensis*)

Moth orchids (*Phalaenopsis* × spp.): These glamorous orchids are surprisingly easy house plants. Tovah Martin says, "Anyone with a well-lit, west-facing sill and a modicum of humidity can grow a moth orchid."

Scented geraniums (*Pelargonium* spp.): At the Logee homestead, coconut-scented *P. parviflorum* hangs in a basket in a south window in the kitchen. Other scents include nutmeg (*P. fragrans*), apple (*P. odoratissimum*), and spicy 'Logeei', all compact basket types. Avoid giant peppermint and grape-leaf geraniums for the windowsill; they are too robust.

Selaginella: Mossy selaginellas are favorites of Melitta Collier's. They are an excellent addition to terrariums.

Planted for Winter

For winter effect, you need trees for line and pattern; you need round shapes and cones, mounds and vase shapes. You also need plenty of green and touches of brighter color to enliven the scene without disrupting the naturally restrained color harmonies of the season.

Plants that accomplish these goals are arranged in the following categories: needled evergreens and broadleaf evergreens; deciduous shrubs with interesting shapes and branching habit; shrubs and small trees with colored bark and twigs or clusters of bright berries; ornamental grasses, which provide upright, flaring shapes and spiky shapes among the mounds, rounds, and cones of the shrubs and trees; and perennials with rigid stems and flower heads.

NEEDLED EVERGREENS

Dwarf Korean fir (*Abies koreana* 'Starker's Dwarf'): Nest shape with glossy green needles. Zone 4.

Hinoki cypress cultivars (*Chamaecyparis obtusa* 'Crippsii'): Dense cone shape with bright yellow foliage. Zone 6.

Golden sawara cypress (*C. pisifera* 'Golden Mop'): Mound shape, golden yellow. Zone 5.

Juniper (*Juniperus scopulorum* 'Gray Gleam'): Silver-gray, upright form. Excellent winter color. Zone 3.

Juniper (*J. squamata* 'Blue Star'): Metallic plum-gray in winter. Low growing in neat circular form. Zone 4.

Juniper (*J. virginiana* 'Emerald Sentinel'): Deep green, pyramid shape. Zone 2.

Microbiota decussata: Attractive, ground-hugging branches like arborvitae. Turns a lovely bronze in winter. Zone 2.

Dwarf Alberta spruce (*Picea glauca* 'Conica'): Dense, tidy cone shape. Zone 4.

Dwarf blue Colorado spruce (*Picea pungens* 'Hunnewelliana'): Blue needles on a compact pyramidal plant. Zone 4.

Dwarf blue Colorado spruce (*P. pungens* 'glauca globosa'): Rounded shape, blue needles. Zone 2.

Dwarf Colorado spruce (*P. pungens* 'Mrs. Cessarini'): Bright green needles on a dwarf plant of mounding habit. Zone 2.

Procumbent Colorado spruce (*P. pungens* 'glauca Procumbens'): Large, low growing with blue needles. Zone 2.

Golden mugo pine (*Pinus mugo* 'Aurea'): Dwarf, rounded, turns golden in winter. Zone 3.

Contorted white pine (*P. strobus* 'Contorta'): Interesting shape, twisted needles. Zone 3.

Weeping white pine (*P. strobus* 'Pendula'): Graceful, drooping branches. Zone 3.
Golden Scots pine (*P. sylvestris* 'Aurea'): Golden-yellow needles. Zone 4.
Weeping hemlock (*Tsuga canadensis* 'Pendula'): Weeping form. Zone 3.

BROADLEAF EVERGREENS

Korean boxwood (*Buxus microphylla* var. *koreana* 'Wintergreen'): Good green winter color. Other cultivars are 'Winter Gem' and 'Winter Beauty'. Dense, rounded shrub. Zone 4.

Boxwood (*B. sempervirens* 'Vardar Valley'): Dark green color holds through winter. Zone 4.

Bearberry cotoneaster (*Cotoneaster dammeri*): Leaves turn purplish green in winter. Red berries, but not numerous. Prostrate shrub. Zone 5.

Japanese holly (*Ilex crenata*): Several cultivars. Dense, compact shrubs, all with small, shiny evergreen leaves. Zones 5–6.

Inkberry (*Ilex glabra*): Globe shaped, with dark green, shiny leaves. Zone 5.

Meserve holly (*Ilex × meserveae*): Several cultivars. Classic prickly leaves of a gleaming dark blue-green. Scarlet fruits. Pyramid form, up to 15 feet. Zone 5.

American holly (*I. opaca*): Medium green foliage. Red fruit. Becomes a large, pyramidal tree. Zone 5.

Longstalk holly (*I. pedunculosa*): Smooth elliptical leaves. Showy red fruits dangle on long stalks. Large shrub or small tree. A favorite of Polly Hill's. Zone 5.

Mountain laurel (*Kalmia latifolia*): Several cultivars. Dark green elliptical leaves do not curl in the cold weather. Zone 5.

Drooping leucothoe (*Leucothoe fontanesiana*): Graceful mound of drooping branches with morocco-red winter foliage. Zone 5.

Oregon grape holly (*Mahonia aquifolium*): Hollylike leaves turn purplish in winter. Blue fruits persist into December. Low, broad, dense mound. Zone 6. Also *M. bealei*: Giant hollylike leaves touched with red in winter. Large, upright shrub. A favorite of Joanna Reed's. Zone 6.

Japanese andromeda (*Pieris japonica*): Several cultivars. Red drooping flower buds through the winter. Shiny evergreen leaves. Zone 5.

Cherry laurel (*Prunus laurocerasus* 'Otto Luyken'): Gleaming dark green foliage on a compact form. Takes pruning. Tolerant of shade. Zone 6.

Evergreen azalea, Nakaharae group (*Rhododendron*): Hybrids of *R. nakaharae*.

Low, dense mounds of small, shiny leaves two feet high or less. Winter foliage in shades of green and bronze-red. Look for Polly Hill's cultivars: 'Joseph Hill', 'Michael Hill', 'Pink Pancake', 'Wintergreen', 'Marilee', 'Susannah Hill'. Zone 5.

Himalayan sweetbox (*Sarcococca hookeriana*): Low-growing evergreen with shiny foliage. Insignificant flowers appear in very early spring and are fragrant. Zone 6.

Japanese skimmia (*Skimmia japonica*): Shiny foliage on a low-growing plant. Terminal clusters of small bright red fruits on female plants. Fruits ripen in fall and persist all winter. Zone 7 (6 in a sheltered place).

DECIDUOUS SHRUBS

Red-twig dogwood (*Cornus stolonifera*): Dark red stems. The cultivars 'Flaviramea' and 'Green and Gold' have yellow stems. Zone 2.

Burning bush (*Euonymus alatus*): Wider at the top than the bottom; the branches form a fan shape. Attractive ridged bark. Small red fruits split open and show orange seeds. Zone 4.

Witch hazel (*Hamamelis* × *intermedia*): Several cultivars. A vase-shaped small tree or multistemmed shrub. Very early blooming. Wispy four-petaled yellow, orange, or red flowers. Some are fragrant. Zone 5.

Sweetspire (*Itea virginica* 'Henry's Garnet'): Mound of gracefully arching stems, reddish in winter. Dark red foliage lasts into December. Zone 5.

Winter jasmine (*Jasminum nudiflorum*): Green whiplike stems bear small yellow flowers whenever the weather warms up during the winter. A favorite of Jack Dunbar's. Zone 6.

Kerria (*Kerria japonica*): Mass of upright, arching green stems in winter. Zone 4.

Star magnolia (*Magnolia stellata*): Large shrub or small tree with beautiful gray bark. Fuzzy flower buds are a winter attraction. Zone 3.

Stewartia (*Stewartia ovata*): A large shrub or small tree with mottled bark in shades of gray and tan. Zone 5.

Korean stewartia (*S. koreana*): A small tree with beautiful patterned bark. Zone 5.

Highbush blueberry (*Vaccinium corymbosum*): Handsome, twiggy winter silhouette. Oriental in feeling. Zone 3.

Spirea (*Spiraea* × *bumalda* 'Anthony Waterer'): A neat, dense shrub with a pleasing twiggy form and papery dried flower heads. Zone 3.

Alpine spirea (*S. japonica* var. *alpina*): Very low mound of dainty twiggy stems. Nice winter shape. Zone 3.

Red chokeberry (*Aronia arbutifolia*): An upright multistemmed shrub. Clusters of red berries persist into winter. Zone 4.

Japanese barberry (*Berberis thunbergii*): Several cultivars. Tight, twiggy, prickly shrubs with bright red oval berries. Zone 4.

Cotoneaster (*Cotoneaster horizontalis*): Attractive fishbone branches lie close to the ground. Red berries. Zone 4.

Heart's a-Burstin' (*Euonymus americanus*): Large native shrub with astonishing fruits in October. Joanna Reed says they are "like bright pink candy popcorn." Zone 5.

Winterberry (*Ilex verticillata*): Polly Hill cultivars: 'Earlibright', 'Bright Horizon', 'Quansoo', 'Tiasquam', 'Aquinnah', 'Chickemmoo'. Dark-stemmed, upright, twiggy shrub. Twigs are crowded with red and red-orange fruits. Zone 3.

Bayberry (*Myrica pensylvanica*): Twiggy, upright shrub of medium height bearing waxy gray berries. Zone 2.

Firethorn (*Pyracantha coccinea*): A stiff, thorny shrub with gorgeous orange-red berries. Zone 6.

Staghorn sumac (*Rhus typhina*): Growth habit like wide-spreading antlers; bears terminal clusters of dark red, suede-textured berries. Zone 3.

Rugosa rose (*Rosa rugosa*): Forms a thicket of spiny canes with urn-shaped orange hips. Zone 2.

Tea viburnum (*Viburnum setigerum*): Showy clusters of red berries on an upright shrub. Zone 5.

American cranberry bush (*Viburnum trilobum*): A tall, upright shrub with decorative scarlet berries that hold well into winter. Zone 2.

Mapleleaf viburnum (*V. acerifolium*): A low, suckering shrub with blue fruits. Zone 3.

ORNAMENTAL GRASSES

Not all ornamental grasses hold their shape in the face of snow and rain, but those listed here are winter winners. Unless noted, they turn shades of parchment, tan, and golden beige.

Feather reed grass (*Calamagrostis* × *acutiflora* 'Karl Foerster'): Narrow, upright flower plumes. Zone 4.

Northern sea oats (*Chasmanthium latifolium*): Attractive flat, oatlike flower heads. Zones 3–4.

Plume grass (*Erianthus ravennae*): Very tall plumes reach 15 feet. Zone 4.

Blue oat grass (*Helictotrichon sempervirens*): Beautiful pale blue blades form a neat spiky clump 2 feet tall. My favorite low grass for winter interest. Holds its blue color in the winter. Zone 4.

Giant maiden grass (*Miscanthus floridulus*): 12 to 15 feet tall, with large plumes. Zone 6.

Maiden grass (*M. sinensis* 'Gracillimus'): One of the best — a fountain of straw-colored, narrow leaves, curly silver-beige seed heads. Zones 4–5. Also *M. sinensis purpurascens:* Purple cast to the leaves. Zone 4.

Switch grass (*Panicum virgatum*): An airy winter beauty. Zone 3.

Fountain grass (*Pennisetum alopecuroides*): Another wonderful winter grass. Graceful mound of fine, straw-colored blades and fuzzy caterpillar flower heads. Zones 4–5.

For other grasses that enhance the winter garden, consult Carole Ottesen's splendid book, *Ornamental Grasses: The Amber Wave.* See Further Reading.

EVERGREEN PERENNIALS

These plants retain their foliage and have a very long season of attractiveness because of their durable, good-looking leaves. Their effectiveness in the winter garden depends to some extent on the weather.

Carpet bugle (*Ajuga reptans*): Generally stays handsome; rosettes of dark green to bronze leaves. Zone 3.

Arum italicum 'Pictum': Beautiful large arrowhead-shaped leaves with white veins. At 20° F, stems lie down, but as soon as it warms up a little, the foliage is as attractive as ever. Zone 6.

European ginger (*Asarum europaeum*): Shiny, kidney-shaped leaves. Zone 4.

Bergenia (*Bergenia cordifolia*): Large paddlelike leaves take on red tints in winter. Zone 3.

Pinks (*Dianthus* spp.): Several cultivars. Spiky mats of silver to blue-gray foliage. Zone 4.

Hellebore (*Helleborus* spp.): Three species for cold climates: *orientalis,* which has shiny palmate leaves; *niger,* which has very dark green, matte-finish palmate leaves on a less vigorous plant; and *foetidus*, which has finely segmented palmate leaves of a dark green. Zone 3.

Perennial candytuft (*Iberis sempervirens*): Mops of finely cut foliage, more or less evergreen. Zone 3.

Lily turf (*Liriope muscari*): Strappy, arching leaves are either green or variegated gold and green. Tough and attractive. Zone 5.

Creeping phlox (*Phlox subulata*): Spiky low mats of muted green. Zone 2.

Christmas fern (*Polystichum acrostichoides*): Evergreen fronds lie down in a mound in winter but stay a good dark green. Zone 4.

Hens-and-chicks (*Sempervivum* spp.): Like small, solid sculptures, plants turn shades of gray, gray-green, and plum-green. Zone 4.

Lamb's ears (*Stachys byzantina*): Furry silver-white leaves stay decorative until they become sodden. In a dry, open winter, they remain attractive until spring. Zone 4.

Thyme (*Thymus* spp.): Low mats of tiny leaves that stay green or turn gray-blue to blackish green. Zone 4.

Yucca (*Yucca filamentosa*): A wonderful spiky accent for the winter garden, especially the variegated cultivars with glowing golden-striped swordlike leaves. Zone 4.

PERENNIALS WITH INTERESTING SKELETONS

Any perennial with rigid stems can add structure to an otherwise flat winter flowerbed.

Astilbe cultivars: Stiff stems topped with pointed flower heads. Zone 4.

Calamint (*Calamintha nepeta*): A puff of threadlike stems. Zone 5.

Threadleaf coreopsis (*Coreopsis verticillata*): A stiff network of fine stems. Zone 3.

Coneflower cultivars (*Echinacea purpurea*): Black cones like knobs at the top of stiff, branched stalks. Zone 3.

Russian sage (*Perovskia atriplicifolia*): Gray, gracefully curving stems. Zone 5.

Black-eyed Susan (*Rudbeckia fulgida*): Stiff, branching stems with black button-shaped seed heads. Zone 3.

Sedum 'Autumn Joy': Large flat flower heads form platforms for caps of snow. Zone 4.

Planted for the Birds

A high proportion of plants in the United States that provide birds with winter food are, of course, native, but many have exotic counterparts with similar fruits or seeds. Some of the native plants are in cultivation as garden subjects. Others are not, but can be used in a garden setting. All are valuable to birds and other wildlife.

The symbol N means that the plant has been ranked high or very high in value for wildlife by Gary Hightshoe, the author of *Native Trees, Shrubs and Vines for Urban and Rural America*. Asterisks (*) indicate that the plant is especially valuable for attracting birds; the more asterisks, the more species the plant attracts.

TREES

N**   Fir (*Abies* spp.): Good cover, seeds inside cones. especially *A. balsamea,* Zone 2; *A. concolor,* Zone 2; *A. lasiocarpa,* Zones 2–3. Cones hang on throughout winter.

N   Maple (*Acer* spp.): Seeds.

N   Hazel alder (*Alnus rugosa*): Fruits persist throughout winter. Attracts songbirds, waterbirds.

N**   Birch (*Betula* spp.): Especially gray birch (*B. populifolia*). Attracts waterbirds, grouse, prairie chickens, chickadees, purple finches, redpolls, yellow-bellied sapsuckers, pine siskins, sparrows.

N*   Common hackberry (*Celtis occidentalis*): Songbirds. Zone 3.

N**   Dogwood (*Cornus* spp.): *C. florida* is especially popular but soon denuded of fruit.

N*   Hawthorne (*Crataegus* spp.): Attracts songbirds, especially robins (in the spring), cardinals, cedar waxwings. Fruits persist.

N*   Persimmon (*Diospyros virginiana*): Fruits ripen in late fall, hang on through winter. Attracts songbirds, upland game birds.

N*   Beech (*Fagus grandifolia*): Small nuts attract songbirds, upland game birds.

N***   Eastern red cedar (*Juniperus virginiana*): One of the best. Berries last through the year. Upland game birds and songbirds — bluebirds, catbirds, crossbills, finches, flickers, grosbeaks, jays, sapsuckers, starlings, tree swallows, thrashers, thrushes, warblers, and, in the spring, robins, mockingbirds, and cedar waxwings. Zone 3.

N   Eastern larch (*Larix laricina*): Songbirds. Seeds in cones throughout the year.

N*   Crab apples (*Malus* spp.): Especially those with small fruits. Important to returning migratory birds in spring, especially robins.

N*   Spruce (*Picea* spp.): Seeds in cones, edible needles. Attracts songbirds, especially crossbills, chickadees, grosbeaks, nuthatches, pine siskins, cedar waxwings.

N**   Pine (*Pinus* spp.): Seeds in cones, edible needles. Attracts many songbirds and also grouse, doves, pigeons, prairie chickens, quails, turkeys.

N**   Oak (*Quercus* spp.): The staff of life in winter for many songbirds, waterbirds, waterfowl, and upland game birds.

N*   Sumac (*Rhus* spp.): Not a favored food, but an important survival food. Berries persist all winter. Attracts upland game birds, songbirds.

N   Hemlock (*Tsuga* spp.): Provides good cover. Cones with seeds through winter. Important food for pine siskins, crossbills, chickadees, blue grouse.

N*   *Viburnum* spp.: Especially *V. prunifolium*, Zone 3. Persistent fruits. Attracts upland game birds and songbirds.

SHRUBS

N   Common alder (*Alnus serrulata*): Cones with seeds. Zone 5.

N   Indigobush (*Amorpha fruticosa*): Capsule with seed. Attracts waterfowl, marshbirds, shorebirds. Zone 3.
        Leadplant (*A. canescens*): Attracts upland game birds, songbirds. Zone 2.

N   Bearberry (*Arctostaphylos uva-ursi*): Important to grouse, northern upland game birds. Also enjoyed by bears!

N   Chokeberry (*Aronia* spp.): Fruit through December. Attracts songbirds, upland game birds.

N   Buttonbush (*Cephalanthus occidentalis*): Nutlets persist through the winter. Attracts waterfowl, marsh- and shorebirds.

N   Summersweet (*Clethra* spp.): Seeds attract songbirds, upland game birds, shorebirds, waterbirds.

N**   Gray dogwood (*Cornus racemosa*): According to Michael A. Dirr, author of

A Manual of Woody Landscape Plants, "over 100 birds supposedly savor the fruits."

N   Wintergreen (*Gaultheria procumbens*): Very limited number of users, but important to grouse and turkeys in winter for persistent red berries. A West Coast species is used by grouse, pigeons, and songbirds.

N   *Hypericum* spp.: Seeds attract songbirds, waterbirds, upland game birds.

N**   Winterberry (*Ilex* spp.): Persistent berries attract songbirds (especially bluebirds, cardinals, mockingbirds, robins, and thrushes), wild turkeys, upland game birds.

N**   Juniper (*Juniperus* spp.): Berries attract songbirds and ground birds.

N**   Northern bayberry (*Myrica pensylvanica*): Persistent berries attract many kinds of songbirds, waterfowl, shore- and marshbirds, including ducks, grouse, quail, turkeys, bluebirds, catbirds, chickadees, crows, flickers, grackles, meadowlarks, thrashers, titmice, towhees, vireos, warblers, woodpeckers, and wrens.

N**   Bristlecone pine (*Pinus aristata*): Seeds in cones attract upland game birds and songbirds.

N**   Scrub oak (*Quercus ilicifolia*): Tops the food list for many songbirds, game birds, waterbirds.

N**   Fragrant sumac (*Rhus aromatica*): Winter food for upland game birds and songbirds.

N*   *Rosa* spp.: Those with with small hips are best — *R. carolina, R. setigera, R. palustris, R. virginiana.* Attract songbirds and upland game birds.

N   Spiraea or meadowsweet (*Spiraea* spp.): *S. alba* attracts upland game birds; *S. corymbosa* and *S. tomentosa* attract songbirds, marshbirds, and waterbirds.

N*   Common snowberry (*Symphoricarpos albus*): Persistent berries attract songbirds and upland game birds.

N**   *Viburnum* spp.: All are high on the list for wildlife and ornamental uses. Fruit of *V. trilobum, V. acerifolium,* and *V. dentatum* persist into winter. Attract songbirds and upland game birds and provide food for returning migratory birds.

GARDEN PERENNIALS

Leave the following plants standing through the winter to provide seeds for songbirds and ground-feeding birds.

Ornamental grasses
Native prairie grasses and sedges
Hyssop
Rudbeckia
Coreopsis
Mullein
Asters
Sunflowers (annual)
Cosmos (annual)

A small patch of grain — rye, wheat, sorghum, oats, millet — can provide both food and cover for ground-feeding birds and songbirds.

Making It Through the Winter: Dye Plants

In her book *A Weaver's Garden*, Rita Buchanan describes the idyllic summer she once spent in the mountains of Colorado trying out natural dyes. "I had my spinning wheel, and I made a little fireplace outdoors. Every day I spun a skein of wool yarn and gathered a different kind of flowers or leaves to try. Each evening I lit a fire and cooked up a dyebath, added the yarn, and went to bed. The yarn simmered until the fire went out and then cooled off overnight." A self-described "slug-abed," Rita found herself jumping up first thing in the morning to see each new color. "That's the lure of dyeing, the fascination of making colors, and I'm hooked on it," she says.

The following dye plants are all good garden plants as well.

FOR YELLOW, ORANGE, AND GOLD SHADES

Dyer's chamomile or golden marguerite (*Anthemis tinctoria*): Perennial.
Dyer's coreopsis (*Coreopsis tinctoria*): Annual.
Safflower (*Carthamus tinctorius*): Annual.
Garland or edible chrysanthemum (*Chrysanthemum coronarium*): Annual.
Cosmos (*Cosmos sulphureus*): Best cultivars are 'Diablo' and 'Sunny Red'. Annual.
Dahlias (*Dahlia* spp.): Tender tuberous perennial.
Weld or dyer's mignonette (*Reseda luteola*): Annual or biennial.

Goldenrod (*Solidago* spp.): Perennial; supplies a good yellow.
Marigolds (*Tagetes* spp.): Annual; provides yellow and gold shades.
Tansy (*Tanacetum vulgare*): Perennial.
Zinnias (*Zinnia* spp.): Annual.

FOR RED SHADES

Lady's bedstraw (*Galium vernum*): Hardy perennial from Europe, naturalized in the Northeast.
Pokeweed (*Phytolacca americana*, a.k.a. *P. decandra*): Vigorous native perennial.
Madder (*Rubia tinctoria*): Perennial, native to the Mediterranean region.

FOR BLUE SHADES

Indigo (*Indigofera tinctoria, I. suffruticosa*): Tropical shrub that can be grown from seed as an annual or as a pot plant. Rita Buchanan recommends starting one plant in a six-inch pot or three in a twelve-inch pot, setting them outside in the summer, and keeping them in a south-facing window in the winter.
Dyer's woad (*Isatis tinctoria*): A biennial, but harvested for dyeing in the first year. Buchanan grows woad in rows in the vegetable garden.
Dyer's knotweed (*Polygonum tinctorium*): A warm-weather annual that should be grown like sweet peppers.

FOR GREEN SHADES

Black-eyed Susan (*Rudbeckia hirta*): Annual or biennial. Flowers produce a dark olive green.

Note: Most greens are the result of a two-step process. Yarn or wool is dyed yellow first, then dyed blue.

Cut and Dried: Plants for Drying

Some flowers are easy to dry and hold their garden color well. Betsy Williams of the Proper Season says, "Try drying any flower that strikes your fancy. You would be amazed how many flowers retain a semblance of their shape and a great deal of their color. You can start in the spring with forsythia. You can also gather and spread out to dry daffodils, tulip petals, and hyacinth blossoms."

When Sarah Milek of Cider Hill was deeply involved in the business of drying flowers for her wreaths and arrangements, she had a list of fillers, which she called "the basics." She valued *Artemisia ludoviciana* 'Silver King' for its beautiful gray leaves; baby's breath for its airy sprays of tiny flowers; sea lavender, another frothy addition to bouquets; pearly everlasting for its clusters of small white flowers; and love-in-a-mist for its interesting, balloonlike pods.

Fillers like baby's breath and sea lavender air-dry easily and well. Cut them just before the flowers open and make small bunches by tying a few stems together. Hang the bunches upside down in a warm, dry place. Avoid hanging them against a wall. Good air circulation is important. Other flowers are better dried in sand, borax, or silica gel.

The majority of flowers suitable for drying can be air-dried. However, it is worth repeating Betsy's advice: "Take several pieces of one kind of plant material or a certain type of flower. Try it air-dried; try it in the microwave [microwave ovens often come with instruction booklets that include directions for drying flowers and herbs]; try it in the oven; try it in silica gel; try it in sand; try it in kitty litter. See which way works best. Some dry better one way and some dry better another. Length of time depends on the method and on the specific flower. Remember that no two flowers are alike."

EASY FLOWERS FOR DRYING

Bear's breeches (*Acanthus spinosus* var. *spinosissimus*): Perennial. Zone 7.

Yarrows (*Achillea* spp.): Perennial. Zone 3.

Lady's mantle (*Alchemilla mollis*): Perennial. Zone 3.

Ornamental onion (*Allium* spp.): Bulbs and rhizomes. Try *A. christophii*, Zone 4; *A. giganteum*, Zone 5; *A. schoenoprasum* (chives), Zone 4; *A. sphaerocephalum*, Zone 4.

Love-lies-bleeding (*Amaranthus caudatus*): Annual.

Winged everlasting (*Ammobium* spp.): Annual.

Pearly everlasting (*Anaphalis margaritacea*): Perennial. Zone 3.

Mugwort (*Artemisia lactiflora*): Perennial. Zone 4.

Artemisia 'Silver King' (*A. ludoviciana*): Perennial. Zone 5.

Astilbe (*Astilbe × arendsii*): Perennial. Zone 4.
Celosia (*Celosia cristata* types: plumosa and spicata): Annual.
Larkspur (*Consolida ambigua*): Annual.
Globe amaranth (*Gomphrena globosa*): Annual.
Baby's breath (*Gypsophila paniculata*): Perennial. Zone 3.
Strawflower (*Helichrysum bracteatum*): Annual.
Liatris (*Liatris spicata*): Perennial. Zone 3.
Sea lavender (*Limonium latifolium*): Perennial. Zone 3.
Statice (*Limonium sinuatum*): Annual.
Love-in-a-mist (*Nigella damascena*): Annual.
Goldenrod (*Solidago* spp.): Perennial. Zone 3.
Lamb's ears (*Stachys byzantina*): Perennial. Zone 4.
Mullein (*Verbascum* spp.): Perennial, biennial. Zone 5.

HERBS FOR POTPOURRI

The traditional way of making potpourri was to layer partially dried plant material in a crock with salt and store it for two weeks. This method gave rise to the name "potpourri," which means "rotten pot." The modern method is much easier. Pick herbs and roses at the peak of their perfection on a warm, dry morning after the dew has evaporated. Remove the petals from the roses and the leaves from the herbs, arrange them on screens or trays in the shade, and let them air-dry.

There are many different recipes for potpourri. The majority call for a high proportion of rose petals, and all require the addition of spices such as cinnamon, cloves, allspice, and nutmeg. The fragrance in potpourris comes largely from bark, roots, seeds, leaves, and a few drops of professionally produced flower oils. A fixative is added to preserve the natural scents. The most common fixative is ground orris root, available from some drugstores and garden centers. Use two tablespoons for each quart of dried flower petals and herb leaves.

Betsy Williams, who is working on a book about potpourri, has this to say about using flowers as an ingredient: "Any flower suitable for drying is a welcome addition for color and texture, but not many blossoms retain their fragrance after drying." Old-fashioned roses and lavender are among the few exceptions. However, the leaves of the following herbs are valuable aromatic additions to potpourri.

Lemon verbena (*Aloysia triphylla*): Tender perennial.
Calamint (*Calamintha nepeta*): Perennial. Zone 5.

Sweet woodruff (*Galium odoratum*): Perennial. Zone 3.

Bay (*Laurus nobilis*): A tender evergreen tree from the Mediterranean.

Lavender (*Lavandula angustifolia*): Perennial. Zone 5.

Peppermint (*Mentha* × *piperita*): Perennial. Zone 3.

Bee balm (*Monarda didyma*): Perennial. Zone 4.

Sweet cicely (*Myrrhis odorata*): Perennial. Zone 4.

Sweet marjoram (*Origanum majorana*): Annual.

Oregano (*Origanum vulgare*): Perennial. Zone 3.

Scented geraniums (*Pelargonium* spp.): Tender perennials. 'Mabel Grey' is recommended for long-lasting scent.

Rosemary (*Rosmarinus officinalis*): A shrub of Mediterranean origin. Tender perennial.

Sage (*Salvia* spp.): *S. clevelandii,* tender perennial, and *S. officinalis,* perennial, Zone 3.

Thyme (*Thymus* spp.): Perennial. Zone 5.

Selected Readings

Inner Resources

HousePlant
c/o HousePlant, Inc.
P.O. Box 1638
Elkins, WV 26241

An informative quarterly magazine with an extended section in each issue devoted to hydroponics. U.S. $19.95, Canada $22.95. Highly recommended by Melitta Collier.

Kenyon, Stewart. *Hydroponics for the Home Gardener.* Toronto, Ontario: Key Porter, 1992.

Martin, Tovah, guest ed. *Greenhouses & Garden Rooms.* New York: Brooklyn Botanic Garden, 1990.

———, guest ed. *A New Look at Houseplants.* New York: Brooklyn Botanic Garden, 1993.

———. *Once Upon a Windowsill: A History of Indoor Plants.* Portland, Ore.: Timber Press, 1988.

————. *The Well-Clad Windowsill.* New York: Macmillan, 1994.

Proctor, Rob. *The Indoor Potted Bulb.* New York: Simon and Schuster, 1993.

Planted for Winter

Dirr, Michael A. *Manual of Woody Landscape Plants.* Champaign, Ill.: Stipes, 1975.

Glasener, Erica, guest ed. *The Winter Garden.* New York: Brooklyn Botanic Garden, 1991.

Ottesen, Carole. *Ornamental Grasses: The Amber Wave.* New York: McGraw-Hill, 1989.

Springer, Lauren. *The Undaunted Garden.* Golden, Colo.: Fulcrum, 1994.

Verey, Rosemary. *The Garden in Winter.* Boston: Little, Brown, 1988. An English book for an English climate but useful for ideas and inspiration.

Planted for the Birds

Hightshoe, Gary. *Native Trees, Shrubs and Vines for Urban and Rural America: A Planting Design Manual for Environmental Designers.* New York: Van Nostrand Reinhold, 1988. Karen Bussolini's favorite book for researching plants attractive to birds.

Martin, Zim, and Nelson Martin. *American Wildlife and Plants: A Guide to Wildlife Food Habits.* New York: Dover, 1961.

Proctor, Dr. Noble. *Garden Birds: How to Attract Birds to Your Garden.* Emmaus, Pa.: Rodale, 1986.

Stein, Sara. *Noah's Garden: Restoring the Ecology of Our Own Back Yards.* Boston: Houghton Mifflin, 1993.

The Audubon Society Guide to Attracting Birds. New York: Scribner's, 1985.

Holmes, Roger, and Rita Buchanan, eds. *Taylor's Guide to Natural Gardening.* Boston: Houghton Mifflin, 1993.

Tufts, Craig. *The Backyard Naturalist.* Washington, D.C.: National Wildlife Federation, 1988, 1993. Call 1-800-822-9919. National Wildlife Federation, 1400 16th St. NW, Washington, D.C.

Extending the Season

Coleman, Eliot. *The Four-Season Harvest: How to Harvest Fresh Organic Vegetables from Your Home Garden All Year Long.* Post Mills, Vt.: Chelsea Green, 1992. Includes everything you need to know to grow and harvest winter crops. There are directions for everything from building a cold frame to erecting your own hoop house.

The Avant Gardener is an excellent newsletter that regularly publishes special editions devoted to a single theme. The March 1995 issue (Vol. 27, No. 5) concerns ways and means of extending the season, including temporary greenhouses, row covers, hoop houses, cold frames, and other special structures. Order this issue for $2 or a year's subscription for $18 from Horticultural Data Processors, Box 489, New York, NY 10028.

Making It Through the Winter

Buchanan, Rita. *A Dyer's Garden.* Loveland, Colo.: Interweave Press, 1995.
————, ed. *Dyes from Nature.* New York: Brooklyn Botanic Garden, 1990.
————. *A Weaver's Garden.* Loveland, Colo.: Interweave Press, 1987.

The Seed Sowers

Deno, Norman. *Seed Germination, Theory and Practice.* This paperback book is for the horticulturally ambitious. Mr. Deno is professor emeritus of chemistry, Pennsylvania State University, and a passionate rock gardener. He can and does grow anything and everything. Write for his book: Norman C. Deno, 139 Lenor Drive, State College, PA 16801.

Reilly, Ann. *Park's Success with Seeds.* Greenwood, S.C.: Geo. W. Park Seed Co., 1978. A good general reference.

Cut and Dried

Herban Lifestyles
c/o Christine Utterback, editor/publisher
StoneAcre Press
84 Carpenter Road
New Hartford, CT 06057-3003

A delightful newsletter full of herb and plant information and lore. Practical and stimulating. One-year subscription, $18.

Hillier, Malcolm, and Colin Hilton. *The Book of Dried Flowers: A Complete Guide to Growing, Drying & Arranging.* New York: Simon and Schuster, 1986. This is Betsy Williams's favorite book; "I don't think you can beat it for identification," she says. It is a beautiful, instructive, and inspiring book. For drying and arranging, the information is first-rate. However, growing information is for the British climate, as the authors are English.

Loewer, Peter. *The Annual Garden.* Emmaus, Pa.: Rodale, 1988. Although this is not specifically about flowers for drying, it has plans for a garden of everlastings and a splendid, very accessible encyclopedia of annuals. The author identifies flowers for drying — and there are many. He also suggests easy methods. For instance, about love-lies-bleeding (*Amaranthus caudatus*), he says, "The flowers may be cut and dried but don't hang them upside down. Instead, stand the stems upright in a weighted bottle."

Silber, Mark, and Terry Silber. *The Complete Book of Everlastings.* New York: Knopf, 1987. Highly recommended by Betsy Williams as a growing guide for New England and similar climates.

Note: Betsy Williams is working on a book called *The Proper Season,* to be published in 1996. It will describe all the delightful projects with dried flowers that she and her staff engage in.

Getting Together

Barton, Barbara J. *Gardening by Mail: A Source Book.* 4th ed. Boston: Houghton Mifflin, 1994. This wonderful volume is a source of sources. If you have ever fancied *any* plant, you will find listed here a group that caters to like-minded souls. Twenty-five pages are devoted to societies specializing in particular plants. And there is so much more. If you want to know where to find plants, bulbs, seeds, or books, Barbara Barton, a reference librarian and gardener, has done all the work for you. Do you like ferns? Look them up under Plant Sources. You will find a code that tells you where to learn more about a particular nursery's offerings.

Index

Amaranth, 66
Amaranthus caudatus, 179, 185
Amaryllis, 3
American Begonia Society, 16
American chestnuts, 28
American cranberry bush, 66, 171
American Hemerocallis Society, 153
American holly, 27, 169
American Horticulturalist (magazine), 3
American Horticultural Society, 3, 136
American Rhododendron Society, 31
American Woman's Garden, The (Samuels and Verey), 32
Ammobium spp., 179
Amorpha
    canescens, 175
    fruticosa, 175
Amsonia, 141
Anaphalis margaritacea, 179
Ancient gardens, 51–52
Anderson, Victoria, 140, 141
Andromeda, 126, 169
Angel-wing begonias, 166
Anisodontea hypomandarum, 10, 166
Anthemis tinctoria, 177
Aphrodite, 141
Apples, 2, 11, 90, 151–52
Appropriate Energy Technology Small Grants Program, 79
Aquilegia alpina, 126
Arab gardens, 52
Arborvitae, 130
Arctostaphylos uva-ursi, 175
Aronia
    arbutifolia, 171
    to attract birds, 175
Artemisia
    lactiflora, 179
    ludoviciana 'Silver King', 179

Arthur Hoyt Scott Garden and Horticultural Award (Swarthmore College), 31
Arugula, 77
Arum italicum 'Pictum', 172
Aruncus dioicus, 126
Asarum europaeum, 172
Ash, 35
Asian dogwoods, 25
Asparagus fern, 4
Asters, 121, 177
Astilbe
    × *arendsii,* 180
    cultivars, 130, 154, 173
Aubrieta, 121
Autumn ferns, 166
Avant Gardener, The (newsletter), 184
Azaleas
    evergreen, 25, 30, 59, 169–70
    grown by Polly Hill, 25, 26, 28, 29–30
    Kurume, 134
    Nakaharae hybrids, 28, 29–30, 169–70
    North Tisbury hybrids, 28, 30
    as sanctuary for birds, 63
    in suburban gardens, 121

Baby's breath, 141, 179, 180
Baby's tears, 21
Bald cypress, 25
Bamboo palms, 8
Baptisia australis, xiv
Barberry, xiii, 43, 45, 66
Barnard's Inn Farm (Martha's Vineyard), 24-31
Barnes, Albert C., 35–36
Barnes, Laura, 35, 36–37
Barnes Arboretum, 35, 37
Barnes Foundation (Merion, Pa.), 36, 39
Barton, Barbara J., 155

Buckwheat hulls, as mulch, 58
Bulbs
    forcing of, 3, 60
    overwintering of, 3
    in urban gardens, 58–59, 121
Burdick, David, 155, 156–60, 161
Burnet, 13
Burning bush, xvii, 66, 67, 170
Bussolini, Karen, xi, xii, 2–3, 42, 152,
    162, 165
Buttercups, 141
Buttonbush, 175
Buxus
    microphylla var. *koreana* 'Winter
      Beauty', 169
    microphylla var. *koreana* 'Winter
      Gem', 169
    microphylla var. *koreana* 'Winter-
      green', 169
    sempervirens 'Vardar Valley', 169

Cabbage, 103, 105
Cactus, 123
Calamagrostis × *acutiflora* 'Karl Foer-
    ster', 171
Calamintha
    nepeta, 173, 180
    nepeta nepeta, 71
Camellia japonica, 166
Camellias, 18, 26, 58, 59, 62, 166
Campanulas, 94
Candelabra primroses, 116
"Candy carrots," 76
Cane begonias, 8
Cape primroses, 17
Caprilands Herb Farm (Conn.), 144
Cardinals, 65, 69
Carnations, 141

Carolina jasmine, 15, 167
Carpet bugle, 172
Carpinus betulus, xiii
Carrots, 72, 76, 77
Carter, Jimmy, 79
Carthamus tinctoria, 177
Caryota mitis, 167
Caucasian fir, 26
Cedars, xiv
Celeriac, 71
Celery, 105
Celosia cristata, 180
Celtis occidentalis, 174
Central Park Conservatory Garden
    (New York City), xiii, 49
Cephalanthus occidentalis, 175
Cercidiphyllum japonicum, 31
Cercis canadensis, 126
Chamaecyparis
    obtusa 'Crippsii', 23, 154, 168
    pisifera 'Golden Mop', 168
    for visual interest, 23
Chamomile, 141
Charlesworth, Geoffrey, 117–23
Chasmanthium latifolium, 125, 172
Cherry laurel, 59, 169
Cherry tomatoes, 82
Chickadees, 64–65, 69, 106
Chiltern's (England), 124
Chimaphila umbellata, 155
Chinese evergreens, 8
Chinese fan palm, 167
Chinese white cabbage, 82
Chives, 179
Chokecherries, 107, 175
Christmas decorating, 146–52
Christmas fern, 173
Chrysanthemum coronarium, 177

Golden marguerite, 177
Golden mugo pine, 168
Goldenrod, 178, 180
Golden sawara cypress, 168
Golden Scots pine, 169
Gomphrena globosa, 180
Grape arbors, 52, 53
Grapes, 56, 66
Grasses. *See* Native prairie grasses; Orna-
    mental grasses
Gray birch, 174
Gray dogwood, 175–76
Greenhouses, 9–15, 72–73, 76–77, 79,
    80–88, 105, 156–60
Greenhouse window, 2–3
Green Scene (magazine), 79, 81
Ground covers, 33
Grouse, 69
Gymnocladus dioicus, 31
Gypsophila paniculata, 180

Hackberry, 174
Haddad, Sue, 160
Hairy woodpeckers, 66, 69
Hall, Elizabeth, 47, 48
Hamamelis
    × *intermedia,* 170
    × *intermedia* 'Diana', 58
    mollis, 34
    vernalis, 34
Hanging Gardens of Babylon, 7, 51
Hardy Plant Study Group, 154
Hawks, 69
Hawthorne, 174
Hazel alder, 174
Hazelnuts, 151–52, 162
Heart's a-Burstin', 171
Hedera helix, 10

Hedges
    as boundaries, 41, 42, 45, 54, 66
    maintenance of, 39
    openings in, 43
Heirloom houseplants, 19
Helichrysum
    bracteatum, 180
    as a houseplant, 11
    in urban gardens, 58
Helictotrichon sempervirens, 43, 172
Helleborus
    foetidus, 33, 173
    as a houseplant, 49
    niger, 172–73
    orientalis, 172
    recommended varieties of, 172–73
    in urban gardens, 59
    for visual interest, 33
Hemlock, 69, 175
Hens-and-chicks, 173
Herbal medicines, 138
Herbal Treasures, 140
Herban Lifestyles (newsletter), 67, 68, 185
Herbert, Vincent, 158
Herb gardens, 13, 51–56
Hermannia verticillata, 15
Heuchera, 154
Highbush blueberry, 170
Hightshoe, Gary, 174
Hill, Joseph, 30
Hill, Julian, 29, 30, 31
Hill, Polly, xiii, 24–31, 169, 170, 171
Hillside Gardens (Norfolk, Conn.), 128
Himalayan sweetbox, 170
Hinoki cypress cultivars, 168
Hollies
    to attract birds, xvii
    'Blue Maids', 60

Rex begonias
  'Firmament', 16, 166
  hydroponic growth of, 8
  Logee's hybridization of, 16
Rhapis excelsa, 167
Rhododendron
  carolinianum, 126
  maximum, 34
  nakaharae, 28, 29–30, 169–70
  nakaharae 'Joseph Hill', 30, 170
  nakaharae 'Late Love', 30
  nakaharae 'Marilee', 30, 170
  nakaharae 'Michael Hill', 30, 170
  nakaharae 'Nakami', 30
  nakaharae 'Pink Pancake', 30, 170
  nakaharae 'Susannah Hill', 170
  nakaharae 'Wintergreen', 30, 170
Rhododendrons
  to attract birds, 63
  from the Far East, 134
  grown by Polly Hill, 25, 28, 29–30
  grown from seed, 126
  in urban gardens, xii, 59
  in woodland gardens, 34
Rhus
  aromatica, 176
  to attract birds, 175
  typhina, 66, 171
Rice, 7
River birch, 24
Robins, 66
Rockefeller, John D., Jr., 146
Rock gardening, 121–23
Rodale Company, 81
Roe, Pinkie, xvii, 131–37, 162
Rogers, Betsy, 49
Rokujo, Tsuneshige, 29, 30
Root and Radish Club (Marblehead, Mass.), 154

Roper, Lanning, 48
Rosa
  'Bonica', 130
  carolina, 176
  'Cecile Brunner', 18
  'Fairy', 100
  glauca, 126
  'Heather', 142
  palustris, 176
  rugosa, 171
  setigera, 176
  'Sterling Silver', 142
  'Thérèse Bugnet', 45
  'Tiffany', 142
  virginiana, 176
Rosehips, 44, 151, 152
Rosemary
  grown in a greenhouse, 10
  in potpourri, 12
  recommended varieties of, 181
  topiary of, xv, 9, 158
Roses
  to attract birds, 176
  climbing, 56
  dried, 141, 142, 180
  miniature, 58
  rugosa, 171
  shrub, 13, 94
  wild, 107
  for windowsill gardens, 18
  winter color of rosehips, 44
Rosmarinus officinalis, xv, 9, 10, 181
Rubia tinctoria, 178
Rudbeckia
  to attract birds, 177
  fulgida, 173
  hirta, 178
  for visual interest, xiv, 13
Rushmore, Robert, 122

Vaccinium corymbosum, 170
Verbascum spp., 180
Verey, Rosemary, 32
Viburnum
    acerifolium, 171, 176
    to attract birds, xvii, 64, 66, 175, 176
    dentatum, 176
    introduced by Chinese Wilson, 134
    prunifolium, 175
    recommended varieties of, 171
    setigerum, 171
    trilobum, 66, 171, 176
Victoria (magazine), 141

Walls
    retaining, 51, 54
    of stone, 25–26, 34, 94
    in Sumerian gardens, 51
Ward, Nathaniel, 19
Water
    for birds, 64
    in garden design, 55
    for irrigation, 51–52
Watering, 18, 159
Wax begonia, 4
Weaver's Garden, A (Buchanan), 112–13,
    115, 177
Weeping beech, xii-xiii, 56
Weeping hemlock, 169
Weeping white pine, 169
Weld, 109, 177
Well-Clad Windowsills (Martin), 17
Wheaten wreath, 151
White birch, 24
White cedar, 97
White pine, 107
Wiley, Molly, 135, 136

Williams, Betsy, xvii, 97, 139–46, 154,
    178-79, 180
Williams, Ned, 140, 142, 143, 144, 145–46
Wilson, Ernest Henry ("Chinese"), 134–
    36, 162
Wilson, Joseph Lapsley, 36
Windbreaks, 79
Windowsill gardening, 17, 103
Windy Hill Nursery (Great Barrington,
    Mass.), 156
Winged everlasting, 179
Winter aconites, 34
Winterberry, 66, 106, 171, 176
Wintergreen, 176
Winter jasmine, 58, 162, 170
Winter projects, 96–115
Witches' brooms, 105
Witch hazel, 34, 58, 136, 170
Woad, 109, 112, 178
Wolfe, Mary Lou, 81
Wood anemones, 107
Woodland gardening, 33–34, 35, 104–5
Woodruff, 141–42
Wreath of Christmas Legends, A (Wil-
    liams), 140
Wright, Frank Lloyd, 61

Yarrows, 141, 142, 179
Year-round gardening, 70–88
Yellow-twig dogwoods, 45, 170
Yews, xiii, 42, 45, 59, 63
Yucca filamentosa, 173

Zinnias
    dried, 141
    as a dyeplant, 178
    as houseplants, 9
    recommended varieties of, 178